Gender Equality In Church Ministry

A Study of the Acceptance of
Women in Church Leadership

Dr. Beverly Barnes-McDonald

DEDICATION

To my beloved husband, Deacon Don E. McDonald, without whom this journey would not have been possible, you have been there as a cheerleader, friend, and confidant, and you are truly the wind beneath my wings. To my children, Lena L. Pettway, James F. Barnes, and David M. Barnes, thank you for always being there for me. To my eight grandbabies, Taylor A. Pettway, James F. Barnes, Jonathan R. Barnes, Bradly S. Pettway, Austin Chester Barnes, Zackary C. Pettway, Solomon A. Barnes, and Ebony S. McDonald, I love you all. Also, to my deceased parents, Mrs. Loree Carter and Mr. Solomon Shepard, Jr., my siblings, and other family and friends who have prayed for me and kept me focused, I am grateful to you for all of your love and support. To all of you, this book is affectionately dedicated.

The late Dr. Echol L. Nix, Jr. and I shared a timeless bond as mother, son, and mentor. He was as one of my own sons. His contributions to my dissertation project were significant and much appreciated. I was blessed to have him always encourage me to keep writing, pushing, and being my best. The printed copy of my dissertation arrived in the mail the day he left us. He is one of the persons to whom I dedicate this project. I will miss his "How you doing, Mama?" As well as the wisdom, love, and support he so freely gave our entire family. His fingerprints can be traced in the DNA of my project and the core of my heart. He will be forever missed.

TABLE OF CONTENTS

DEDICATION............ iv

FOREWORD 1

GLOSSARY 4

ACKNOWLEDGEMENTS 6

ABSTRACT 8

INTRODUCTION 9

CHAPTER I.. 13

CHAPTER II 24

CHAPTER III.. 44

CHAPTER IV 71

CHAPTER V 87

CHAPTER VI.. 128

APPENDIX A 139

APPENDIX B 143

APPENDIX C 151

APPENDIX D.. 158

BIBLIOGRAPHY... 164

FOREWORD

D r. Beverly McDonald's, Gender Equality in Church Ministry is one of the most significant researched, data-driven, and personal first-hand experiences from a black female in ministry. With permission given by the senior pastor of Bethel Baptist Church, Pratt City, Birmingham, Alabama, Dr. McDonald utilized this Church as her content of study. Dr. McDonald invested her time, heart, passion, love for God, and determination in exploring and researching the root cause(s) of her hypothesis: If female ministers at Bethel Baptist, Pratt City, receive training on gender equality in ministry, then their knowledge of gender equality would increase.

Dr. McDonald is a woman of integrity, honesty, a lover of God, and a strong supporter of equal rights and equality for all humankind but primarily women, which is her subject of discussion.

Dr. McDonald and I met in Seminary. We often talked about finding the meaning in our lives as women in ministry under strong, hierarchical, and male domineering leadership. The pastoral work we do for God is significant as it involves loving and caring for others. We found the courage to push forward even through difficult times of being oppressed, suppressed, under-valued, and told we could not preach or teach nor hold the office of a pastor because we are women. Through it all, this phenomenal woman of God, Dr. McDonald, has proven beyond the shadow of a doubt that ministry will forever be the center of her heart. This book displays her determination to help the body of Christ by "righteously dividing the Word of God" and bringing clarity and meaning from the Scripture through the work of the Holy Spirit.

Dr. McDonald's hypothesis, research, and findings in this study are as follows, "If the female ministers at Greater Calvary Missionary Baptist Church in Birmingham, Alabama receive training on gender equality in ministry, then their knowledge of gender equality would increase. The researcher used a mixed-methods approach, and the result of the evaluation of this study is a null hypothesis. When female ministers at Greater Calvary Missionary Baptist Church in Birmingham, Alabama, received training on gender equality in ministry, little change in knowledge or attitudes was observed."

Dr. McDonald's research included various disciplinaries who presented their findings through presentations and proof from Scriptures. Dr. McDonald included statistical data from different male and female multiple age groups and ministerial/civilian vocations. This research has opened people's eyes and hearts to learn more about God's plans for men and women in ministry. This research has helped me realize how easy it is to become indoctrinated in a particular way of believing and interpreting the Scriptures related to male and female roles in ministry. The Scriptures are proof of God's revelation of equality for humankind. But it is so vital that Scriptures are interpreted correctly. God gave the woman a "voice" in Jesus's conception, His early ministry, death, burial, resurrection, and throughout the Bible.

There is no blame game, but there should always be a willingness to learn and educate oneself and trust God in the process. God said, "Trust in the Lord with all thine heart; and lean not to our own understanding." Proverbs 3:5. I commend Dr. McDonald for her remarkable research and well-written book. I believe that life is meaningful, and I know she agrees; we all have a part to play in it. We are all made equal in the sight of God. God is the originator of the call to all humankind. And for that, I am grateful unto Him.

Pastor, Chaplain Debbie Williams, MDiv, CA, GC-C

GLOSSARY

1. Church ministry—The activity and responsibility of the local church in the fulfillment of its biblically defined mandate in the world.

2. Five-fold ministry gifts—The specific roles that Christ gave the local church in Ephesians 4:11-12.

3. Gender bias—Unfair difference in the way women and men are treated.

4. Gender equality—A set of actions, attitudes, and assumptions that provide opportunities and create expectations about individuals; the process of allocating resources, programs, and decision-making fairly

to both males and females without any discrimination on the basis of sex and addressing any imbalances in benefits available to males and females [66].

5. Greater Calvary Missionary Baptist Church- A pseudonym for the context of this study. The church is situated in the Northwest section of Birmingham, Alabama.

6. Humanity—The human race.

7. Spiritual gifts—The means of transmitting the powerful and purposeful divine presence into the flesh and blood of humanity. The two-fold ministry where the church ministers to itself for health, wholeness, and edification for service [14].

8. SPSS—Statistical Package for the Social Sciences; a software package used for the analysis of statistical data.

9. Pastor—A shepherd in spiritual and jurisdictional charge of a congregation or church.

10. Minister—Anyone authorized to carry out or assist in the spiritual functions

ACKNOWLEDGEMENTS

The writer wishes to express her appreciation to the core faculty and staff of the Doctor of Ministry Program, Virginia University of Lynchburg. To President Kathy C. Franklin, Ph. D. and Executive Dean, Graduate School of Religion, Leonard N. Smith D. Min., thank you. She will always be grateful to Dean, Graduate School of Religion, Marshall D. Mays, D. Min. Director, Doctor of Ministry Program and Core II Reader, James E. Coleman, Jr. D. Min, her Core Faculty Advisor, Carlton Jackson, D. Min., Core Faculty Advisor, Philip Campbell, D. Min., Administrative Assistant, School of Religion, Brenda H. Morton, D. Min. and Administrative

Assistance, School of Religion, Mrs. Delphine Mickles.

Gratitude and appreciation are also expressed to the members of the candidate's committee, Melissa Buckley, Ph.D., Zelda Kitt, Ph.D., Echol L. Nix, Jr., Ph.D., Rev. Gilbert Tyler, D. Min., Peer, and Rev. Geraldine O. Moore, MRE, Contextual Associate. Without their expertise, insight, and assistance, this project would not have been completed, nor would it have been as meaningful. The candidate is also appreciative to her pastor, Dr. Tommie L. Lewis, the Bethel Baptist Church, Pratt City, and all of the other contextual associates and participants who gave their time, assistance, and feedback to support this project. Special thanks to the writer's granddaughter, Taylor A. Pettway, for her formatting and typing and Alexia N. Terrell for assisting with the graphs and charts to interpret the statistical data.

Most of all, the candidate thanks Almighty God for His loving kindness and tender mercy. It has been Him who has kept her, inspired her, and liberated her through this awesome experience.

ABSTRACT

GENDER EQUALITY IN CHURCH MINISTRY

Greater Calvary Missionary Baptist Church in Birmingham, Alabama is the context of this study. The hypothesis of this study is as follows: if the female ministers at Greater Calvary Missionary Baptist Church in Birmingham, Alabama receive training on gender equality in ministry, then their knowledge of gender equality would increase. The researcher used a mixed-methods approach. The result of the evaluation of this study is a null hypothesis. When female ministers at Greater Calvary Missionary Baptist Church in Birmingham, Alabama received training on gender equality in ministry, little change in knowledge or attitudes was observed.

INTRODUCTION

Throughout history, racism and sexism have been issues in the workforce and the church. The writer has personally observed and experienced pronounced, unfair, and unequal practices both in ministry and in her professional life. As a female minister, the writer feels a distinctive call to help both males and females embrace the liberating truth of God's Word where both genders are equally accepted and appreciated.

The culprit of this injustice lies at the heart of a quasi-inclusive church culture where male dominance, gender bias, and inaccurate analysis of scripture prevail against sound doctrinal practice and spiritual equality. Dr. Edward Wimberly explains that behaviors are learned and often passed down from one generation to the next [94]. In his D. Min. dissertation entitled Eradicating Gender Bias in Church Leadership, Dr. Ernest Burroughs further states "that the church does not look at nor view women like they do men, which is a big issue, especially in the Baptist church [15]."

> Women have been denied equal opportunities in ministry, unlike their male counterparts.

The title of this research project is "Gender Equality in Ministry." Greater Calvary Missionary Baptist Church in Birmingham, Alabama, is a neighborhood church established in 1897 and has experienced both growth and challenges, culminating in its current status in the community and surrounding areas. Here, the writer currently worships and serves in various leadership capacities. It is also here that the writer would like to positively impact the ministry experience of other females who labor in spreading the gospel of Jesus Christ.

The researcher has observed that women have been denied equal opportunities in ministry, unlike their male counterparts and many ministry activities are well-defined and restricted. Her goal is to find a way to alleviate some of the social ills and problems that plague her context, the ecclesia as a whole, and society today. Knowing that gender roles or the lack of equality between men and women in ministry play an important part in this dilemma, this writer is deeply troubled by the difference in treatment of female preachers versus their male counterparts, especially in the South.

As a Black female minister, the writer sees Christ as a liberator, and although she is concerned with man's salvation, she is also worried about their oppression. Dr. James Cone [20], a Black Liberationist, writes, and the researcher paraphrases, "salvation should not be a passive inward calmness or invisible cure in the life to come; thus, it no longer acts like a harmful drug in support of racism." But that God, through His Son Jesus the Christ, saves humanity by entering the depths of their pain and oppression [45].

This dissertation documented the implementation of the project proposal. It was developed to train female ministers on gender equality in ministry in the hope that their knowledge of gender equality would increase. Seeing through different lenses helped the participants conceptualize the research with broadness and depths of scope. Through this dissertation project, the researcher will enable the readers to see that racism and sexism are equally detrimental to our society and the church. This dissertation will have six enlightening chapters.

Chapter I, Ministry Focus, will look at the marginalization of Black women and allow the reader to examine the researcher and her motives in delving into this topic. The focus is on Greater Calvary Missionary Baptist Church in Birmingham, AL, a progressive church on the move for God. Its motto is: "A Bible-Based, Christ-Centered, Holy-Spirit Lead and Mission-Bound Church."

Chapter II, State of the Art in this Model of Ministry, will

11

examine the related books, articles, interviews, and other sources used to develop the ministry model.

Chapter III, Theoretical Foundation for the Model, will address the Biblical texts used in the ministry focus. It seeks to give the reader Biblical Scriptures, history, psychological and social consideration for this study.

Chapter IV, Methodology, will discuss the design of the ministry model used in the candidate's project. It will allow the reader to view the goal of the hypothesis and the methods used to design the ministry model. It will also discuss the timeline development and the lesson plans for each lesson.

Chapter V, Field Experience, will describe each training session and how it helped equip the participants to understand gender bias and its impact on society. This chapter will also explain what was accomplished and what went wrong in the sessions.

Chapter VI, Summary, Reflections, and Conclusion, will summarize the project's accomplishment and show what the researcher learned from the project and the researcher's journey. It will provide reflections, conclude the findings, and share the writer's mistakes and failures with the reader.

CHAPTER I
MINISTRY FOCUS

Black women, with their communal spirits and dignity, have made great sacrifices both in society and in the church. They built schools, ran social programs, and extended aid wherever there was a need. While of great value, research on women preachers does not capture the more representative role of the majority of women church members. If taken alone, such discussion renders women's roles marginal. Left unheard are women's voices within the public discourse of racial and gender self-determination [38]. Thus, women must seek to develop their voices.

Blacks have been denied access to public spaces, such as parks, libraries, restaurants, meeting halls, and other public places. The Black church marginalized women just as whites had done to people of color. Even though women make up the majority of the congregation, Black women in most denominations face gender inequality. Masculine bias was and still is, in many cases, evident in institutions structured by men.

The writer has observed through historical church records that since the inception of Greater Calvary Missionary Baptist Church—which is the context of the ministry of the writer—female ministers have been denied equal opportunities in most aspects of ministerial duties, which include performing communion, training for the pastorate of local congregations, and officiating weddings, baptisms, and funerals. The culprit of this injustice lies at the heart of a quasi-inclusive church culture where male dominance, gender bias, and inaccurate analysis of scripture prevail against sound doctrinal practice and spiritual equality. While good intention and strong conviction beg to maintain the status quo, change is needed. Currently, women are denied the opportunity to grow, share, and preach as their male counterparts solely based on their anatomical design. As a result, female spiritual leadership is limited, female pastorates are all but denied, and complete inclusions into some ministry activities are well-defined or restricted. To date, Greater Calvary Missionary Baptist Church has not had a female pastor in its history. While some female ministers enjoy the opportunity to be licensed, only two have been ordained – of these two, one minister's ordination was transferred from another church.

This issue not only presents restrictions for the female preacher, but it is a disadvantage for those who would otherwise benefit from her ministry. The parishioners and male ministers also suffer from the lack of diversity and administration of gift sets from a female minister. For example, there are approximately eighteen sitting ministers in the ministry context, twelve of whom are female. The disproportion of male ordinations versus female ordinations speaks to

> To deny a female preacher the opportunity to minister to her God-graced capacity freely denies her a voice.

the accessibility of males to further their ministry as pastors and not having to continue to sit in waiting. Many of the males who were a part of the ministry were immediately courted to pastor churches, leaving the female ministers behind to wait as sitting ministers. This phenomenon exists beyond the scope of the context of this ministry and extends to related churches within the district, local, state, and national conventions with similar practices and beliefs.

Although the ability to exercise one's gift is important in advancing the Kingdom of God, the ability to have a voice is critical in any and every setting. To deny a female preacher the opportunity to minister to her God-graced capacity freely denies her a voice. Denying such a fundamental civil right undercuts social and civil justice that has taken years for our country to obtain. Subsequently, the religious sector which propagates liberty has become an institution of imprisonment by its archaic, male-dominant practices against women in ministry.

The writer acknowledges that her life's experiences in the corporate world have influenced her heightened sensitivity to male dominance and inequality. The candidate retired from civil service as an Ordnance Officer (a specialist in bombs, bullets, grenades, rockets, etc.). That career field was not only predominately White but also predominately male. The candidate's resolve was solidified while growing up in the South and working in this discriminating environment. She was determined to make some contribution to alleviating gender inequity.

The researcher has spent her life advocating for social justice and equality for all people, particularly people of color and women, as she represents both groups. Her professional life has allowed her to gain insight from working in a male-dominated workforce where she was subjected to racism, bigotry, and gender bias. Lessons learned from her experiences have increased her awareness and seasoned her voice as a Black female. She answered the call to go just as Isaiah 6:8, "Who shall I send and who will go for us, [43]" and has become one of the two ordained female ministers in the ministry context. While she has enjoyed expressing her gifts in this ministry, she has also experienced inequities. She has seen first-hand the difference in treatment of female ministers compared to her male counterparts.

One of the ways the writer has combated the issue was by developing her knowledge of the Word of God through seminary studies. She has observed that most misunderstandings and cultural behaviors are based on scriptures, making women inferior and

16

subservient to men. Through years of formal research, her knowledge and insight of scripture have allowed her to deepen her understanding and expand her personal view of God's ability and desire to use women in all aspects of ministry. This personal knowledge gives her a unique vantage point to the current problem. The vision of this plan is to experience true liberty in church ministry for all people. This is especially so for female ministers. As a student of Dr. James Cone and a proponent of Black Liberation Theology, the writer knows that a vision realized means liberation for future generations even more than for one's self.

The Black church has long suffered abuse and mistreatment in the name of Christianity. As current as in 2017, Charlottesville, Virginia, served as an example of such juxtaposition of faith. White men who believed that God created them to be of a superior race took to the streets of this great state to declare that faith gives them the right to do as they think and yet remain in right standing with God. Many LGBT communities protested against this behavior and understood this march to be a march against equality for all, including the gay community. History records such women as Mrs. Rosa Parks, Mrs. Claudette Colvin, Ms. Jo Ann Robinson, Mrs. Georgia Gilmore and Mrs. Johnnie R. Carr had courage and determination in Montgomery, Alabama, and stood up against injustice, inequality, and segregation. It was the same in Birmingham, Alabama, where Mrs. Helen Shores Lee, Mrs. Barfield Pennington, Mrs. Annie B. Peterson, Mrs. Connie Goldby, Mrs. Novelle Wilson, and Mrs. Minnie Gaston gave of themselves during the Civil Rights Era to ensure equality for all. There were female foot soldiers in Selma, Alabama, like Mrs. Nancy Gardner Sewell, Mrs. Amelia Boynton Robinson, Mrs. Richie Jean Jackson, and Mrs. Anne Cooper. They were leaders in their own rights that significantly contributed to equality for people of color. The same level of suppression and oppression toward a people exists in the Black church. Male leaders with misogynistic and sexist mindsets declare that they have the God-given authority to stand behind a pulpit and pastor. At the same time, the female must remain subservient in nature and position.

The writer remembers numerous encounters in the cooperate world where she had to stand against inequality, sexism, racism, and bigotry. She knew if she did not stand, those who would come behind her would face a greater challenge. The nation has somewhat evolved in the corporate world. Most families in America enjoy two household employees—both male and female—in the church; it is yet an old battle masked in faith. It may even be the same family where women are equal in the workforce but must be subservient in the church. Politics and religion have long ago married, and its children resemble the benefit of the majority race and sex. Both sex and race majorities are changing, and so must our practices in the church. In particular, the Black church has been long carried by the influence and commitment of female service. In many cases, the female occupies and makes up the majority of its congregation; however, the senior church leadership reflects a different picture. When female leadership is proportionate to male leadership in the ministry context, and when conversations are honest and transparent about the process of getting there, the researcher's vision will be realized.

For Greater Calvary Missionary Baptist Church, the context of the ministry, the church leadership would have more female ministers being ordained and church leaders helping to prepare those female ministers who express interest with the training necessary for both leadership and pastorate. Another significant change would be the willingness to freely minister in all aspects of ministry for all ministers—both male and female alike. The "good ole boy" practices of the inner circle would change to include females in different activities. Considerations would be given to the different needs of both sexes regarding attire and family obligations; however, women would be extended the same opportunities and respect as men.

> Are ministry leaders willing to lose a few followers in hopes of liberation for all?

Another significant change would be to consider a female becoming senior pastor. In the history of Greater Calvary Missionary Baptist Church, they have never had the honor of having a female pastor. The idea has never been fully welcomed as a subject of conversation. When the researcher's goal is achieved, people will be open to discussing female leadership in the senior pastorate as a viable option. This change would require the parishioners and leaders to be accepting and to be willing to value the gift set of a female in key leadership roles.

The ministry context could change in adverse ways as well. As with any change, not everyone would be on board. The probability of losing members is a real possibility. Regardless of the truth presented, some may be simply unwilling to accept change. The question would become, "Are ministry leaders willing to lose a few followers in hopes of liberation for all?" Another possibility is for others who have similar beliefs to join the ministry. One unintended result may be female ministers beginning to flock to other ministries in hopes of an opportunity. This can be either positive or negative for the ministry. Ministry protocols would have to be developed to help potential ministers navigate the learning and development phase to become ordained ministers of the gospel and/or future pastors or any senior leadership role she may feel compelled to serve.

The researcher acknowledges that her ministry context will change. The major difference will then shift to continuing the conversation of equality and maintaining a balance between spiritual liberation, which is defined as "freedom in Christ equal to all," or feminism, which in this context, refers to the "empowerment of women." The writer does not prescribe to a feministic ministry approach; rather, she promotes and advocates for the spiritual liberation of all people. When the vision is realized, it is important to the writer that females understand that the push is not to suggest that women are superior nor that men are superior, rather it is to say as it does in Ephesians 4:5, that there is but one Lord, one Faith and one Baptism. It is to reaffirm the gospel of Jesus, which declares that there is neither gender nor racial difference in God. There is neither Jew nor Gentile, neither slave nor free, nor is there male and female, for you are all one in Christ Jesus (Galatians 3:28). While exegesis of the scripture refers to all having equal salvation regardless of race, gender, or status, the writer believes this is a truth that may be applied to the contemporary church regarding roles in ministry.

The writer is convinced that one's mortal bodies do not empower the ministry of the Holy Spirit; rather, bodies are but carriers of the Truth. Hence, it is the allowance of the Holy Spirit to minister through available vessels, whether male or female. Therefore, the nature of one's anatomical design cannot claim ownership or rights to the Spirit of the Lord. When ministers preach or teach, they must be led by the Holy Spirit. They are to surrender and submit their bodies for the use of the Lord. This is the message the writer hopes the ministry context will espouse once the vision is truly realized.

The writer also knows that her calling is in the process of fulfillment as her destiny in God comprises of more than the liberation of female ministers within her ministry context. She believes that this achievement and its success will become a catalyst for similar ministries. She believes God has ordained her in this age for this specific assignment and that generations to come will reap the blessings of this engagement. She hopes her relationship with other ministers, including key male leaders, would help propagate her message to other contexts who would otherwise dismiss this argument altogether. She believes it is by the design of God to gain the trust and confidence of other ministers, both male and female, on this subject to help advocate for change.

The writer has observed and experienced pronounced unfair and unequal practices in ministry which continued to promote male dominance. As a female minister, the writer feels a distinctive call to help both males and females embrace the liberating truth of God's Word where both genders are equally accepted and appreciated.

The writer also imagines that this change will be personal for her. All her life, she has endured the oppression of sexism, racism, and misogyny in both the workforce and in the Black church. She has been an advocate of human rights and civil liberty and a strong supporter of the gospel of liberation. Her life can easily be summed up as momentum in the making for female ministers in the Black church. She prays for the realization of a strong argument under Black Theology of Liberation—that is, to reach full humanity without obstacles blocking the goal of becoming human beings who can freely do God's will [45].   She prays that this project will be the jolt needed to catapult the writer in the heart of her calling. This change may mean that she will publish articles, continue studies and have opportunities to speak to others about this process and its impact on both the leaders and its parishioners. This change will free the writer to focus on improving the process and helping others to incorporate similar change within their ministry context. The writer will feel complete as having made a significant impact on her world and church. Self-actualization is a powerful tool and can be readily accessed for the writer by achieving this goal.

Greater Calvary Missionary Baptist Church has evolved in

some of its practices and acknowledgments, allowing females to preach and minister from the pulpit podium; however, restrictions still prohibit women from advancing to senior leadership roles. Such restrictions have created glass ceilings for women who aspire to senior leadership roles and responsibilities in the church. While this behavior is rich in traditional views of female roles in the church, many who held this view were ministers who were not taught through a formal ministry institution; instead, several of such practices and teachings were passed down from one generation to the next. In most cases, this view of women being "weaker" paralleled the view of the role of women outside of the church.

The writer has observed other female ministers subjected to similar treatment. This propelled the writer into her calling as she sought God on how such inequalities might yet exist in an era of global evangelism and tolerance. It became poignant and clear that while God's plan is for full acceptance, there are yet customs and cultures allowed to triumph rather than the allowance of the liberating gospel of Jesus to prevail. To this end, the author seeks to impact change within her context and the culture.

CHAPTER II

THE STATE OF THE ART IN THIS MODEL OF MINISTRY

Acts 2:17 (KJV)

And it shall come to pass in the last days, saith God; I will pour out of my Spirit upon all flesh: and your sons and your daughters shall prophesy, and your young men shall see visions, and your old men shall dream dreams

While there is scant empirical data on the equality of women's roles and responsibilities in church ministry compared to men's roles and responsibilities, current research on the topic is through lived experiences and perceptions. Much of the existing literature reflects lived experiences told through various narratives or a form of exegesis of scripture from a particular lens. Researchers agree that the fundamental question to prescribed beliefs about women's roles and responsibilities and of men's roles and responsibilities in the church is the view of creation. The four lenses through which this question is answered are categorized as 1. Traditional. 2. Complimentary. 3. Pluralist, and 4. Egalitarian [17].

Steve Calagna, in his Theological Position Paper, describes the traditional view as one that believes that men and women were created to have different roles. This view holds that men were created to lead and have authority, and women were created to be man's helpers, thus his subordinates.   The second view is referred to as the complementary view of male leadership. The difference between this view and that of the traditionalist is the belief that women were also made in the image of God and therefore shared equal nature; however, those who hold the complimentary view contend that men have positional authority over women both in the home and at the church. Another view that is opposite in opinion is the pluralist view. It holds that neither sex fully communicates the image of God alone, but when in a relationship together, the pluralistic nature of God is expressed. Men and women have shared equal authority. It is also the belief that male dominance resulted from the fall of mankind in Genesis 3. Ministry calling does not depend upon gender but rather on abilities and gifts given by the Holy Spirit.

Finally, the fourth view is called the egalitarian view. Again, the belief is that both males and females were created to exercise equal authority, but male dominance resulted from the fall as recorded in Genesis. It is also believed that Christ restored women to their rightful place of authority through the Holy Spirit and re-established equality among the sexes. Whereby men and women serve according to gifts and abilities and not according to gender.

The question of headship, submission, and equality in scripture is another conversation piece. "In the Evangelical Christian community, the issue of headship, submission, and equality lies at the heart of the fundamental differences between two major proactive groups in the ordination debate." Again, the argument centers on one's view of creation. Richard Davidson, in Women in Ministry: Headship, Submission, and Equality in Scripture [22], notes five major views in the history of scripture interpretation. First, the subordinate woman; second, reaffirmation of subordination as a blessing and comfort to women; third, subordination of women after the Fall; fourth, evil consequence was not a creation ordinance; and fifth, subordination of women as a Creation ordinance. Of these five views, two of these five major views include an idea of hierarchy where women's subordination exists.

In Dr. Evelyn Brooks Higginbotham's book, Righteous Discontent: The Women's Movement in the Black Baptist Church [38], 1880-1920, she explains the role of Black women during the 'woman's era' and "nadir" of race relations of 1880-1920. During the writer's collaboration with Dr. Echol Nix, Jr., one of the candidate's Adjunct Professors made several suggestions regarding the research and especially discussed the importance of Higginbotham's book in any study on Black women in National Baptist Churches. During this period of time of Higginbotham's writings, Blacks were evolving (as our great nation) from slavery and its lasting impact on Blacks, particularly in the South.

> Black women used the Bible to fight for women's rights in both the church and society at large.

According to Higginbotham, Black women used the Bible to fight for women's rights in both the church and society at large [38]. The majority of Higginbotham's writing is centered on the largest group in the Black community-both, both secular and religious—the Baptist church. Her work reveals that Black males understood and encouraged the participation of women in certain aspects of ministry, yet they aimed to silence the voice of women and keep them subordinate, as was the decorum and rules of their organization and beliefs.

Dr. Higginbotham wrote that "the movement gave women the collective strength and determination to continue their struggle for the rights of Blacks and the rights of women [38]." Dr. Higginbotham further stated that "For women disadvantaged by race, gender, and low income at the turn of the century, the conventions annual sessions afforded an opportunity to transcend narrow social and intellectual confines that negated racist and sexist stereotypes and limitations." Dr. Nix further suggested that Baptist women can "find their voice" just as Higginbotham discusses in her book on the role of the Women's

Convention in the National Baptist Church.

Dr. Cheryl Townsend Gilkes builds on the neglected work of historians, and her book, If It Wasn't for the Women: Black Women's Experience and Womanist Culture in Church and Community, supplements studies like Higginbotham's Righteous Discontent. Using historical analyses and sociology, Gilkes examines the Black church and the experiences of women who comprise a large makeup of the church. She especially shows how Black women connect with the community, revealing an emphasis on Black women as community-focused, including in the worship experience, which is both communal and public. Gilkes' depiction of Black women is against the backdrop of racism and sexism—twin evils of contemporary society—and highlights the role and resiliency of Black women despite the odds [31].

Nannie Helen Burroughs, an educator, orator, religious leader, Civil Rights activist, feminist, and businesswoman, whose school in Washington, D.C. now houses the offices of the Progressive National Baptist Convention, greatly influenced this researcher. Her speech to the 1900 National Baptist Convention in Virginia was quite noteworthy as she wrote:

"We come not to usurp thrones nor to sow discord, but to so organize and systematize the work...For a number of years there has been a righteous discontent, a burning zeal to go forward in his name among the Baptist women of our churches...We realize, too, that the work is too great and laborers too few for us to stand by while like Trojans the brethren at the head of the work under the convention toil

28

unceasingly. We come now to the rescue. We unfurl our banner upon which is inscribed this motto, 'The World for Christ. Woman, Arise, He calleth for Thee.' Will you as a pastor…help by not hindering these women when they come among you to speak…? It has ever been from the time of Miriam, that most remarkable woman, the sister of Moses, that most remarkable man, down to the courageous women that in very recent years have carried the Gospel into Tibet and Africa and proclaimed and taught the truth where no man has been allowed to enter. Surely, women somehow have had a very important part in the work of saving this redeemed earth... [16]" Just as Mrs. Burroughs wrote, this writer seeks not to sow discord but to encourage the ecclesia to aid women to rise and answer the "call" of God and go forth with the work that Christ has called women for such a time as this.

Dr. Katie G. Cannon, in her book Katie's Canon: Womanism and the Soul of the Black Community [18], argues through several essay publications "that the women, particularly Black women, were excluded from much Christian literature and rhetoric." Her writings review the hermeneutical distortions of White Christians and uncover the role of the enslavement and dehumanization of African people from any sort of social recognition. Cannon's essay pushed open doors for women in ministry and demanded women's voices, talents, and gifts to be regarded. In the 18th century and early 19th century, Cannon argues that Blacks were stripped of all of their humanity; they were not considered but of a lower nature. Churches and their governing boards agreed to this perception of Blacks, and therefore, Blacks had no socially recognized personhood. The Black church often relegates women to a lower status, just as Whites did for the Black race.

Cannon's essay entitled Hitting a Straight Lick with a Crooked Stick: The Womanist Dilemma and Development of the Black Liberation Ethicist maintains that Black women are not included in the Bible because of the White masculine orientation that characterizes the field of study leaves them out. Dr. Nix thinks that Dr. Cannon's work is foundational for anyone who wants to engage in original and creative scholarship. He also thinks Dr. Cannon is useful considering her work on Phyllis Wheatley, a renowned poet who gave voice to capable, creative intelligence. She wrote: "Through thickest gloom looks back, immortal shade, on that confusion which thy death has made. In every human breast, God has implanted a principle, which we call Love of Freedom; it is impatient of oppression, and pants for deliverance [91]."

Dr. Cannon also discusses the idea of White Christianity as a symbol to maintain control over Blacks. Cannon describes herself as a Black Womanist Liberation Ethicist. Womanism was coined by Alice Walker, a poet, and social activist, as a brand of feminism that included advocacy for women of color. This term expanded the feminist term intending to reach at the intersection of race, class, and gender oppression [9].

Dr. Stephanie Mitchem's book, Introduction to Womanist Theology [62], is a critical source that supplements the work used in my study, referencing Dr. Katie Cannon. Mitchem, like Cannon, explores the unique experiences of Black women. Mitchem, a professor at the University of South Carolina, takes experience seriously and uses it to illustrate what theology is and how theology relates to ethics. Theology is the study of God and God's relationship to the world and human beings. Ethics asks the question, "What shall I do?" Black women are able to analyze church teachings, develop meaningful systems of ethics, and challenge ecclesiastical structures if needed.

Dr. Nix also shared with the writer the work of Dr. Prathia L. Hall, who served as the Martin Luther King, Jr. Professor of Social Ethics at Boston University School of Theology and pastor of Mount Sharon Baptist Church in Philadelphia, Pennsylvania. He and the writer discussed Hall's use of the Black church as the "freedom church" described in Courtney Pace's recent book, Freedom Faith: The Womanist Vision of Prathia Hall [67]. This is the writer's prayer for the ecclesia: just for all to be free to carry out the call of God on their lives.

Dr. Natalie Houghtby-Haddon, in her book Changed Imagination, Change Obedience: Social Imagination and the Bent-Over Women in the Gospel of Luke [40] describes symbolism as an instrument used to form social worlds and meaning which creates a continuing use of one's customs or habits. The author believes that for social groups to share meaning in their world, they must have a common understanding of the symbolism employed within the group. This is especially true for men and women, Blacks and Whites, perhaps understanding each other's truth and being able to view through different lenses.

Dr. Kenneth Hagin, the pioneer of the Word of Faith Movement, addresses the positional authority of women as it relates to a woman's role in the home and church ministry through an exegesis of scripture that he published in a book entitled, The Woman Question [34]. The author points to 1 Corinthians 11:3 to argue that the meaning of spiritual headship is Christ for both man and woman; however, the domestic head of the wife is that of her husband. He points out the wording in the King James Version: "But I would have you know, that the head of every man is Christ; and the head of the woman is the man, and the head of Christ is God." Hagin claims that through critical analysis and review of biblical transliteration, the word woman is actually referring to wife and not the generic term of woman, which signifies that a man has authority over his own wife and not every woman. This argument was foundational for Hagin's later argument, claiming that Christ is the head of all in God, not just the man. From his perspective, he discusses the right of a woman to speak in church and her participation in ministry. One of the culprits that Hagin credits for the error in teaching women's roles is illiteracy and social culture. "Every scripture must be interpreted in the light of what other scripture says on the same subject. It must harmonize with all other Scripture."

Although Hagin asserts the call of God upon the lives of women having all gifts of the spirit, he yet wrestled with women being pastors. He shares guiding notes from P.C. Nelson, a spiritual mentor he described as profoundly impacting his beliefs. P.C. Nelson shared similar beliefs but advised:

32

Shall the heavy hands be laid on such women as God has evidently called and endowed with natural gifts and Gifts of the Spirit? If God hath called them, who are we to recall them? Let God send them forth because He's the one who did it. And when He gets ready to call them in, let Him call them in. I think some men think that they are God, but they are not, and they need to find that out.

Hagin concludes his argument by stating that "there is no place in church that's holier than another. If a woman can teach in the classrooms, she can teach in the sanctuary. If a woman can speak from a platform, she can speak from a pulpit." Finally, Hagin writes about three pivotal scriptures that bear great weight on the subject matter: Acts 2:16-18, Galatians 3: 26-28, and Acts 1:13-14. Through these scriptures, Hagin acknowledges social culture as a culprit for the erroneous teaching of these Scriptures.

According to Hagin, Joel 2:28-"And it shall come to pass afterward, that I will pour out my spirit upon all flesh…." And it speaks of the times of Pentecost and that we yet live in that dispensation, and "all flesh" includes females as it does males. Acts 2:16-18 is then the fulfillment of this Scripture. Verse 17b states: "…and your sons and your daughters shall prophesy…." Hagin argues that women missionaries are sent into foreign places where there are no men to lead them, and they have to teach and preach to men, women, and children. If God can use a female there, why can He not use one here? Hagin addresses this inconsistency by pointing back to the ignorance of Scripture and social customs as hindrances to women being allowed to answer their call and exercise the gift to preach. Hagin concludes with Galatians 3:26-28: For ye are all children of God by faith in Christ Jesus. For as many of you as have been baptized into Christ have put on Christ. There is neither Jew nor Greek, there is neither bond nor free, there is neither male nor female: for ye are all one in Christ Jesus.

Women should be treated just like men, according to scripture. It has been the culture that has driven these customs and practices of non-inclusion.

Dr. Marshall D. Mays, in his book, SERVING TOGETHER: The Pastor and Deacon in Cooperation, Not Conflict [58], said: It is worth noting that within our society, we have female pastors of denominational and non-denominational churches; college and university presidents; female CEOs of business corporations; college and university presidents; female lawyers and heads of law firms; and female superintendents, principals, and teachers overseeing public and private schools and classrooms.

Dr. Mays' book examines women diaconates as servant leaders. He goes on to say that the twenty-first-century church leadership is a mixture of both males and females. Since his book examines women as part of the diaconate, Dr. Mays says that the word diakonos can be both masculine and feminine. Therefore, the scriptures support female deacons within the church.

Expanding the argument of women's inclusion, Dr. Ella Mitchell contends that God caused cultural bias breakthroughs where he demonstrated the inclusion of women equal to that of men in ministry. In her book, Those Preaching Women [60], she cites the records of Deborah, the Israelites' prophet and Judge, and Prophetess Huldah. The author explains that the breakthrough of cultural bias was by means of God's choice of vessels for the Holy Spirit. This argument would extend through the New Testament breakthroughs, where the author shares that Paul s bias was not inspired by God but by his cultural beliefs and experiences. While the author acknowledges Paul as a true Apostle, she examines Paul's admission to saying some things he spoke were by permission and others by inspiration (I Corinthians 7:6).

In her book, Bible Women: All Their Words and Why They Matter [61], Lindsay Harbin Freeman argues that women cover all stations of power as men do in the Bible, just in fewer numbers. The author supports this assertion by listing twelve situations in which women and their deeds were comparable to their male counterparts. For example, she offers: Women were not known as warriors or judges, yet Deborah was both. Women were not known as killers, yet Jael and Judith killed top leaders. Women did not serve as priests, yet when they—including Hannah, Hagar, Rebekah, and Sarah (from Tobit)—cried out in prayer, God answered. Women were not known as diplomats, but the women of Tekoa and the wise woman of Abel were two of the best, and the Queen of Sheba was a skilled and prudent ambassador on behalf of her nation. Women were not named in the twelve-disciple group, but some of Jesus' closest allies were women, including Mary and Martha of Bethany and Mary Magdalene. Women were not known as merchants, but the "good wife" of Proverbs 31 and Lydia in Acts were clearly successful in business. Women were not seen as political advisors, but King Saul sought the witch of Endor (who told him, correctly, that he would die in battle the following day). King Josiah's assistants sought out Huldah to explain the spiritual and political meaning of scrolls, newly found in the temple at Jerusalem.

Women were not seen as prophets, yet Anna recognized Jesus as the long-awaited Messiah when He was only eight days old. Women were not seen as negotiators, yet Abigail negotiated with King David not to slay her household, and the wise woman of Abel negotiated with Joab to save her town. Both were successful. Women were not seen as poets, but some of the oldest and most beautiful poetry is found with women's names attached (the Song of Miriam, the Song of Deborah, the Song of Hannah, and Mary's Magnificat). Girls were not seen as particularly useful, but Jesus' mother was probably about fourteen when she bore him. The servant girl of Naaman's wife suggested a cure for Naaman's leprosy. Pharaoh's daughter saved little Moses while young Miriam stood guard, and Rebekah was just a girl when she greeted Abraham's servant and married Isaac within a few days, sight unseen. Finally, women were not seen as reliable witnesses, but there is the whole Resurrection story, where Jesus did not appear to his disciples first but met the women at the tomb. Freeman's book concluded that being a woman in ancient times was difficult. Women were considered property without rights, voice, or ownership. However, there are the brave actions of many women whose lives are captured in the Scriptures to help readers acknowledge that although the culture and customs of old were mostly focused on men's journeys, the worth of women could not be ignored.

In 2005, Catalyst Inc, a nonprofit consulting group specializing in gender issues, published a report entitled "Women Take Care and 'Men Take Charge: Stereotyping of U.S. Business Leaders Exposed." The report confirms that gender roles are stereotyped in the

> Many female ministers, leaders, and pastors have been hurt and limited by gender stereotypes.

workplace culture. In fact, according to the report, corporate leaders thought women were better at the more relational dimensions of leadership and men at the more strategic dimensions of leadership. Women were perceived as nurturing, caring leaders without the ability or aptitude to take charge. This perspective of women's leadership roles and expectations resulted in reduced advancement into more senior levels of leadership for women regardless of experience and expertise.

Some examples of gender bias in the church are that women are expected to serve in the nurturing roles of children's ministry; rarely do we see or expect men to volunteer in children's ministry. Women are often expected to take on the scribe or administrative roles on church task forces and committees, but men are rarely asked to do the same. Women are mostly absent as speakers at church and national conferences or are present only as psalmists or singers. They do the same work as men yet are given different titles. Women are also often paid less or nothing compared to men in comparable roles or capacities.

Consequently, many female ministers, leaders, and pastors have been hurt and limited by gender stereotypes. Those who subscribe to this stereotype restrict the use of gifts that are graced to females into designated boxes regardless of interest, expertise, or potential. Sadly, the church is often a space where gender bias against women leaders is excused and enabled. If you experience gender bias in church, try the following steps. 1). Keep calm and carry on. 2). Ask questions. Sometimes a belief may be rooted in one's interpretation of Scripture, specifically the Genesis account of God making Adam before Eve. Without getting into a scriptural volleyball match, ask how one reconciled the creation account in Genesis 2 with Genesis 1, where God gave both man and woman stewardship of the earth. Asking questions sometimes provoke others to think about inconsistencies and whether there was any scriptural support for one's beliefs about men and women. 3) Create safe spaces. 4) Examine your lens, and don't be pushy or aggressive. Many Christians still believe that a woman's place is in the home. Both men and women hold these unfounded beliefs [40].

Dr. Zelda Kitt, the researcher's Adjunct Professor I, described her experiences as a female pastor for over twenty-seven years as one filled with challenges between the sexes. She recalled one encounter where the male preachers exited the pulpit because she was invited as guest minister. While the exiting of the pulpit was not aimed to be a personal attack, it was an act of religious indignation of a female preacher occupying the pulpit. She recalled conversations with those men and later learned that two of the men changed their views years after the event, citing that the Lord had called their wives to preach. After they accepted the calling of their wives, they found themselves outside of the circle of their convention and became independent churches.

Another vivid experience Dr. Kitt described was that of female preachers arming themselves with a similar venom of proving the calling of women and bashing men. Dr. Kitt explained that while this group was forming in support of women in ministry, the hurt and offense from their experiences of being denied pulpit ministry acceptance by males and other females became the trending message rather than the gospel of Jesus. For this cause, Dr. Kitt warned others that gender bias might work either way, and either way it works, it is wrong.

Yet more disturbing is an event she shared while traveling to support her pastor. The host pastor invited her into the pulpit, and all seemed to have gone well. During the comments, a visiting minister stood and began to curse the congregation, stating that God was not pleased with this woman in the pulpit and that they were all going to hell for allowing her to sit in the pulpit. Dr. Kitt stated that for the first time, she felt threatened because of the passion and intensity the minister used, pointing and shaking his finger in her face and standing close to her. She remembered the church's deacons standing to their feet and shuffling hands through their pockets. She began to pray, and the choir started to sing. Within minutes the confrontation ended with the minister and his wife abruptly leaving the services. Later, the host minister stood and apologized, stating that "God pours out his Spirit upon all flesh, and your sons and daughters shall prophesy."

The beginning of her ministry was not met without similar challenges. She attended a local Baptist Church in the Birmingham, AL, area. Her pastor's family were members of the Church of Christ, and her pastor's wife's family were all male ministers in the Baptist Church. These men were a part of the Civil Rights Movement and had gained a lot of political and social esteem within the community. When Dr. Kitt shared that God had called her to preach, her pastor refused to allow her. It would take three years of her faithful attendance and submission to his leadership before he would acknowledge her calling. Soon thereafter, the pastor acknowledged that God had also called his wife to preach. At the time, Dr. Kitt did not think that she was an instrument of light for women in ministry, nor did she consider herself fortunate or favored. She understood the struggle and wanted nothing more than to pray and not have to answer the call of God to ministry.

Dr. Kitt shared that she never received much disdain as she did the works of an evangelist—television ministry, radio broadcasts, or literature and tent ministries; however, standing behind the pulpit caused a lot of concern from family and friends and strangers alike. This was true, especially in certain congregations, particularly the Baptist. These attitudes intensified as she founded a church in her

40

community. Pastors would come and try to convince people not to attend. She was called a witch and told she was only there because God could not find a willing man. She endured the ridicule and the isolation for years. Soon she would have secret calls from male pastors requesting her assistance in prayer and the gifts of the Holy Spirit that she possessed. She later understood that while some may not be able to accept her equal to male pastors, nonetheless, they honored her life of giving, praying, and humility before God and others.

Reflectively, Dr. Kirt recognizes that the struggle for equality in ministry is deeply embedded in prejudice. Through no fault of her own, she is female and is called of God. She explains to listeners that she did not believe God should call a woman only to discover that the calling and gifting of God are not about gender but rather His choosing.

Rev. Geraldine Moore, the researcher's contextual associate who actively serves in various leadership capacities in the National Baptist Convention and the affiliated state and local denominational organizations, has personally observed the dual organizational structure, namely separate men and women ministries. However, many times females in the church exhibit a reluctance to accept women ministers as well. She said that the role of females in ministry was constantly debated in the Bible College in which she was enrolled in the late 1980s. Females were not allowed to enroll in homiletics courses during that time; however, today, that has changed.

Rev. Moore stated that there is a vast difference between

41

National Baptist Convention churches and the Methodist denomination, where many females serve as pastors. She mentioned that she had visited the Full Gospel Convention, where women are equally embraced as ministers, pastors, and bishops. She also said that this had been evidenced by the extremely large number of women arrayed in their clergy collars and females who serve in leadership on the Council of Bishops.

Since her call into the Gospel Ministry, she has observed a change in the openness of accepting female preachers. The change has been slow and gradual, but in the words of a popular commercial a couple of years ago, "We have come a long way, baby," but we still have a long way to go! Just as Rev. Moore holds a somewhat different view of the context, the writer knows that there are others with opposing views to her argument. For example, Charles Ryrie, in his book, The Role of Women in the Church [74], says that even though women were present at Pentecost and received the same Spirit as the men, it was a significant fact that activities that were assigned to women were different from those which our Lord assigned to men. Ryrie went on to say that even though Christ publicly taught women, as he did men, their primary function was to minister. Christ ministered to men: but the women ministered to Christ. He also interpreted the Genesis piece as women must be subservient to men.

Mr. Ryrie mentions in his book that "women were perhaps a part of the 120 disciples sent out, they were among the crowd in the upper room, and they were with the group that prayed for Matthias,

Judas's replacement. Priscilla. along with her husband, was mentioned six times in the New Testament, but they were perhaps only helpers," according to Ryrie. Women played an important role in the early church, but to say they played a leading role is another matter. Did they just open their homes to the early church for meeting places?

"Some women like Priscilla, Apphia, Euodia, and Syntyche were doubtless leaders in their respective assemblies, but to say that women played a leading role is another matter. The incarnation was in a man; the apostles were all men: and the chief missionary activity was done by men; the writing of the New Testament was the work of men; and in general, the leadership of the churches was entrusted to men," Ryrie writes [74].

The writer will perhaps be criticized for her stance on gender equality; however, she knows that the time is now to put forth this argument. There must be a change to the status quo. It may not happen in her lifetime, but perhaps something will be said that will catapult the change or make some type of difference, even if it is just dialogue.

Reading Pam Jarrett's book, Now is the Time [46], has strengthened her resolve. Jarrett says in her book, "Don't worry about what people will say, worry about what Christ will say —we've got to get moving doing what God has ordained us to do." She went on to say: pray for boldness, pray for strength, pray for wisdom, pray for His will to be done in your life and in our world.

CHAPTER III

THEORETICAL FOUNDATION

FOR THE MODEL

The Virginia University of Lynchburg's Doctor of Ministry Program, of which this writer is a member, has the following group emphases: the first emphasis is to become imbued with the Philosophy of Self-Help and Interdependence, which seeks to recognize the possibilities in every human being and maximizes the contributions of gifts of the individual within the context of the global community; the second emphasis is to encourage the learner to develop their own authentic postures of self-determination, which will equip the learner with the ability to speak and act freely without fear of the impediments from a malevolent society or culture [85].

Old Testament Scriptures

There are at least seven key Old Testament scriptures and seven New Testament scriptures that the writer draws inspiration for ministry, which informs beliefs and guides practices that will be used in this dissertation paper in terms of curriculum design. Although not mentioned in either order of most importance or least, each scripture presented weighs equally important to the writer regarding this study. The following Old Testament scriptures will serve as discussion items: Genesis 1:27, Genesis 5:1-2, Joel 2:28-29, Judges 4:6-7, 2 Kings 22:13-16, 2 Chronicles 34, and Numbers 2. The following New Testament scriptures will be highlighted as key scriptures: Acts 18:26, Galatians 3:28, John 4:1-42, Acts 10:15, 19, Acts 2:14, and Matthew 28:6.

According to the Bible, God created "them" mankind — meaning both genders. The separation of the species was not qualified by strength or weakness but rather by functionality. So, God created human beings in his own image. In the image of God, he created them, male and female; he created them in Genesis 1:27 (NIV); Genesis 5:2 (NLT). These two scriptures help readers to understand the origin of creation. They reveal God's intent and heart for creation. God created them both and called them both "Adam," which means mankind. This reference is gender-neutral and absent of classism or division. Creation for one purpose of procreation is agreeable; however, culture has impended a far darker meaning, which devalues women's strengths and makes them subservient to men. A cross-reference is made in Matthew

45

9:4, the writer reminds readers, "'Jesus answered, Have you not read that from the beginning the Creator made them male and female'" (KJV).

This scripture is further supported in Genesis 5:1. The author notes that this is the book of the generations of Adam. In the day when God created man, He made him in the likeness of God. Again, this reference to man or Adam simply means human beings or mankind. The word Adam is gender-neutral in Genesis 5:1.

Joel 2:28 (NIV) sheds light on the authority upon which women could and should engage the Holy Spirit in ministry. He states: And afterward, I will pour my spirit on all people. Your sons and daughters will prophesy, your old men will dream dreams, and your young men will see visions. Even on my servants, both men and women, I will pour out my Spirit in those days.

In reference to Joel, 2:28, Kenneth Hagin in The Woman Question [34] critically reflects on this passage found in the Old Testament and the New Testament. He connects Joel 2:28 with Acts 2:16, 17 by establishing the idea of authority in the context of prophesying and preaching, including in the church. For Hagin, prophesying is a "phase" of preaching under the "inspiration of God." Hagin maintains that Joel's prophesy "hundreds of years before the day of Pentecost" was fulfilled on the day of Pentecost." As such, Hagin thinks we still live in what he calls "the Holy Ghost Dispensation," which includes women as well as men. He concludes: "The daughters will prophesy as well as the sons."

This scripture is inspirational as it reminds one that it is the will of God that women are included in the ministry of the Holy Spirit. There are no limits on gender, race, nationality, or age. God has a full inclusion ministry for all people. In Hebrew, the term prophet is "Nabi" from a root meaning to bubble forth; to utter. Anyone being a spokesman for God to man might thus be called a prophet. This term may also refer to a woman as prophetess. It bears the same definition. The term preacher in Strong's Concordance [80] is kerusso (pronounced kay-roo'-so) is to proclaim, to publish, and to herald, especially divine truth (the gospel).

> There are no limits on gender, race, nationality, or age. God has a full inclusion ministry for all people.

An example of how God used women equal to men is found in the book of Judges, chapters 4 and 5. Here is the story of Deborah, the prophetess, and judge. Deborah was called by God and recognized by all as the fourth judge of pre-monarchic Israel—the only female judge named in the Bible. Deborah's judgeship was after the death of Joshua, and she was known to be a prophetess. Deborah's assignment and duties were not swayed because of her anatomical design. Indeed, she was called into judgeship at a time when the Jewish people were greatly distressed under the cruelty of the Canaanites. Amid the torment and evil, Deborah answered the call, and under her leadership, the Jews triumphed over their enemies. Notably, she was courageous in battle. The scripture notates that Barak refused to go to battle without her. Her influence was great, and God's heart was equally open to the need to include women in the victory. Deborah explained to Barak that although he would be victorious, he would not be credited for the victory. Instead, a woman would be honored for this victory. It happened as Deborah prophesied.

This leads the writer to briefly discuss prophecy and its relationship to preaching and pastoring. The purpose of this inclusion is because the readers are to be reminded that the term pastor/preaching is not mentioned in the Old Testament regarding women; however, the term prophesy is mentioned. The writer argues that by definition, the terms may be used interchangeably. It is undeniable that God used women to prophesy; however, for some, this term lacks inclusion to pastor or preach. According to Strong's Concordance [80], the word prophecy is the Hebrew term nebuah (neb-oo-aw) which simply means a prediction (spoken or written). Thayer's Greek Lexicon defines prophecy as "discourse emanating from divine inspiration and declaring the purposes of God, whether by reproving and admonishing the wicked, or comforting the afflicted, or revealing things hidden; especially foretelling future events. Anyone being a spokesman for God to man might thus be called a prophet. This term may also refer to women as prophetesses. It bears the same definition.

To this end, 2 Kings 22:13-16 captures Prophetess Huldah sending a message to the king upon his urge to seek understanding of God about the book of the law that the priest, Hilkiah, found. We discover that although Huldah was married to Shallum, keeper of the

48

wardrobes, the scripture clearly depicts to readers that Huldah's call was recognized by those who feared and sought the heart of God. She was sought after and respected by King Josiah, a scribe and a priest. All three were recognized as authorities on the earth, and two of them were thought to be learned of God. Yet, they sought the anointing of a woman, Prophetess Huldah. Although nothing more is spoken of this woman in the canonized scripture, her presence and her words are powerful. We recognize that not every event is included in scripture; however, including this woman's ministry further confirms God's perception of women being included in ministry. This story is also captured in 2 Chronicles 34.

Another note-worthy scripture from which the author draws much inspiration is that found in Numbers 22:28. "Then the Lord opened a donkey's mouth, and it said to Balaam, "What have I done to you to make you beat me these three times?" While the donkey does not preach, it reveals God's wonder-working power. This one scripture defies what was known to man as natural ability. It contradicts all logic; this type of occurrence is noted only once. However, the implications from the scripture are far-reaching. This scripture confirms what every believer must acknowledge—which is, God, can do as He so desires

In 2 Kings 4: 1-2, 7, the wife of a man from the company of the prophets carried out to Elisha. "Your servant my husband is dead, and you know that he revered the Lord. But now his creditor is coming to take my two boys as his slaves. Elisha replied to her, how can I help you? Tell me what you have in your house? She went and told the man

49

of God, and he said, go sell the oil and pay your debt. You and your sons can live on what is left". God's concern for women was shown through the mercy of the prophet. God empowered the prophet to change this widow from a beggar to an entrepreneur. God sees the needs of all with no gender bias.

New Testament Scriptures

Another scripture, John 4:1-26, gives yet deeper meaning to this theme. In this scripture, we find a woman being commissioned by Jesus to tell others of her encounter with the Lord. The thirsty woman interacts with a Fountain of Life, and her outcome is to tell others. A compelling scripture is recorded in Acts 10:15, 19 (KJV). Peter has a vision whereby the Lord gives him a revelation. Peter receives and shares the revelation that nothing God has created is unclean. Although this scripture points to types of foods, it also speaks to cultural customs and beliefs. The take-away lesson is that anything God has created cannot be called "common." This scripture sheds light on the cultural belief systems that existed among the disciples that were not congruent with the teaching of Christ.

Acts 2:17 is another powerful scripture reference that the writer draws upon. In this scripture, Peter makes references back to Joel 2:28. He preached to the masses to explain the phenomena that the disciples were displaying and pointed them to what the scripture had said in the book of Joel. In The Woman Question [34], Dr. Kenneth Hagin argues that women missionaries are sent into foreign places where there are no men to lead, and they have to teach and preach to men, women, and children. If God can use a female there, why can He not use them here? Hagin addresses this inconsistency by pointing to the ignorance of Scripture and social customs as hindrances to women being allowed to answer their call and exercise the gift to preach. Again, the account of Jesus' resurrection as recorded in Matthew 28:6 shares how Mary and the other women were the first to arrive at the tomb of Jesus and were directed by the angels to return and tell the others that Jesus was not dead but He was resurrected from the dead as promised. Mary and the other women were the first to spread the good news of the gospel of Jesus Christ. Lastly, Philippians 4:3 records Paul urging others to care for the females who "co-labored" in the gospel with him.

Although many other scripture sources inspire and guide the writer's understanding and guide this project, the ones mentioned are indeed the most prevailing. Altogether, these scriptures reveal the heart of God to include females in the ministry in various capacities. Ministry calling does not depend upon gender but rather on abilities and gifts given by the Holy Spirit.

Theological Foundation

God

The writer understands God as the Creator of the universe as recorded in Genesis 1:11. Furthermore, the writer believes that God is the author and Creator of all that exists as recorded in God's Word. "For in him all things were created; things in heaven and on earth, visible and invisible, whether thrones or powers or rulers or authorities; all things have been created through him and for him ." 1 Colossians 1:16

Therefore, the writer believes that God purposefully included a woman in the creation of mankind, Genesis 5:1. The term used for Adam was simply to mean mankind. In this essence, the writer believes that God created Eve equal to Adam, only having a different function for reasons of procreation. However, God created them both in His image and in His likeness; therefore, neither male nor female was superior in function, knowledge, or role. The candidate also believes that no one is comparable to Him, and none existed before Him. According to the Holy Scriptures, God is an eternal spirit, "He is who is, was, and shall be" (Rev 1:8) "…for the eternal God is my refuge." (Deuteronomy 33:27)   The writer understands God to be almighty, all-powerful, omnipresent, omniscient, and all-knowing. He is also a loving shepherd and father who cares for His sheep (Psalms 23). The writer also recognizes God's functionality as the great judge and the avenger of truth (James 4:12). There is none higher in authority; there is none wiser in wisdom or more able in power and might. He is the sovereign God, Colossians 1:17; and Psalm 8:1. Therefore, in the wisdom of God, males and females were made equally in God's image and His likeness. This equality did not change until the fall of mankind, where we begin to see in the Holy Scriptures where Eve is described as inferior, "the weaker vessel," and the blame for the Fall. Neither sex fully communicates the image of God alone, but when in a relationship together, the pluralistic nature of God is expressed [22].

52

Jesus

The writer sees Jesus as The Great Liberator. Even though Jesus is a part of the Trinity, His functionality is that of a Savior, Redeemer, and Liberator. His relationship to God was as Son, yet He functions in complete unison with God, the Father. Jesus came to save and liberate. He left the Holy Spirit to lead, guide, and protect. This liberation came to women as it did to men. The writer understands the significance of Jesus' liberation. Whereas the culture of the era restricted and restrained inclusion in the church, Christ invited all to come and be part of the Kingdom of God. Jesus confronted, challenged, and changed many of the cultural practices that otherwise discounted the value of women. In his book A Black Theology of Liberation [20], Dr. James Cone says that Christ reveals that the liberation of the oppressed is a part of the innermost nature of God Himself. That means liberation is not an afterthought but the essence of divine activity.

This liberation came to women as it did to men. First, a woman was used for His virgin birth to carry Him to life on earth. Although women were not named among His first 12 disciples, women were included in Jesus' ministry. They were among the seventy-two sent out to minister (Luke 10:1-11). Jesus interacted with both males and females. Some women, namely Joanna, Susanna, and Mary, the mother of James, accompanied Jesus and even supported his ministry as men did (Luke 8:1-3). Anna, the prophetess, Claudia, and Dorcas (or Tabitha, depending on the language) were church leaders or

53

evangelists.

Jesus also chose Mary Magdalene to tell the story of His resurrection to His disciples. The Gospel of Luke describes Mary Magdalene's role as equal to a disciple; more is written about the role she played in the ministry of Jesus than any of the other female followers. The writer understands the significance of Jesus' liberation. While during my research, it was suggested by Dr. Nix to study the Gospels in general and the Gospel of Luke in particular because of the special concern for women in Luke's gospel.

Holy Spirit

The working of the Holy Spirit is paramount because Jesus left Him for mankind. If believers but trust, He is the one that guides, enlightens, and keeps us. He doesn't allow us to get too far out of God's will. If we should sin, the Holy Spirit functions as a conviction in our hearts. Romans 8:26 testifies that "Likewise the Spirit helps us in our weakness, for we do not know what to pray for as we ought, but the Spirit himself intercedes for us with groaning too deep for words." He keeps us in alignment with God's Holy Word. His interaction is not always physical. He sometimes works through our mental, psychological and emotional beings. He also teaches us. John 14:26 states, "But the Helper, the Holy Spirit, whom the Father will send in my name, He will teach you all things and bring to your remembrance all that I have said." When the text is read, the Holy Spirit opens our minds and hearts to understand what the text is saying. The Holy Spirit enables and empowers believers to stay the course and finish the journey. Acts 1:8 declares, "But you will receive power when the Holy Spirit has come upon you, and you will be my witnesses in Jerusalem and in all Judea and Samaria, and to the end of the earth." Of all the support, impartations, and comfort offered by the Holy Spirit, the writer takes much consolation from John 16:12-15 - "I still have many

> The church operates from the core belief of the reign of God and thus exemplifies the Lordship of Jesus.

things to say to you, but you cannot bear them now. When the Spirit of truth comes, he will guide you into all truth, for he will not speak on his own authority, but whatever he hears he will speak, and he will declare to you the things that are come. He will glorify me, for he will take what is mine and declare it to you. All that the Father has is mine; therefore, I said that he will take what is mine and declare it to you ."

The writer believes the functionality of the Holy Spirit is indeed relevant because it is by way of God's Holy Spirit that people understand spiritual truths It is also because of the Holy Spirit that mankind can perceive the will of the Father. Revelation is given through the Holy Spirit regardless of cultural bias or beliefs and practices.

Church

The candidate thinks of the universal church as the collection of saints regardless of denomination. This includes all races, genders, denominations, and cultures. It is the Body of Christ consisting of all believers of God the Father, Jesus, the Son, and the Holy Spirit. The universal church is worldwide; however, the local church is a unit of the universal church. It may have denomination affiliation and vary in process, delivery, procedures, and protocols. Also, the local church may interpret certain parts of scripture differently than others, but the centerpiece is the belief in the Holy Scriptures and the Holy Trinity. While the real tabernacle is within the heart of mankind, the local church is an assembly of believers who gather to worship, fellowship and commune with God and share like beliefs about God and the Holy Trinity.

The church is to operate in conjunction with the Kingdom of Heaven as it is God's Kingdom extended here on earth. The writer believes that the church is an extension of God's Kingdom. It is God's reign, and according to Scripture, this is the work of the Cross by which Jesus was crucified and is risen. God's power and authority rest upon each Believer who is in Him; subsequently, the church is a symbol of the collection of saints who are in Christ and submits to the sovereign reign of God. The church operates from the core belief of the reign of God and thus exemplifies the Lordship of Jesus. Hence, God's Kingdom has come upon the church. The church, having such incredible power, is purposed with an equally critical mission as recorded in Matthew 28:19:

Go ye therefore, and teach all nations, baptizing them in the name of the Father and the Son, and of the Holy Ghost.

Historical Foundation

The writer is greatly influenced by Black liberation theology because of its call for justice and equality. Although the author was somewhat sheltered at a young age, she vividly remembers the "Jim Crow" era. She remembers as a young teen not being allowed to ride the bus with friends because there was still residual racism (even after the Montgomery Bus Boycott). She also remembers "White" and "Colored" water fountains and restrooms. In his book, A Black Theology of Liberation [45], Dwight Hopkins emphasizes God as the Creator of African Americans and others to be free and "to reach their full humanity without obstacles blocking the goal of becoming human beings who can freely do God's will." God's divine spirit continues to enable and sustain Black people on our journey toward liberation. Black Liberation Theology is an effort of African-American people to claim blackness and freedom as people of God. It stands to reason that the author would be an active participant in this struggle as a part of the Black ecclesia.

In addition, the candidate supports Womanist Theology. She is a Black woman who identifies with the limits and restrictions placed on women, in general, and those in the church specifically. Conversely, she is not a feminist, strictly defined. However, the candidate believes this helped shape her passion for ministry. The candidate describes her spiritual, theological belief as Pentecostal. Although she is a staunch Baptist, she believes that the hallmark of true Christianity must be a modern experience of Pentecost, which is baptism in the Holy Spirit.

She believes in various gifts of the spirit and modern miracles of the spirit and that the Bible is the definitive authority in matters of faith.

Psychological Foundation

The writer's ministry context is a predominantly African American Baptist church with deep roots in the historical changes of the South with regard to racial, political movements. Na'im Akbar authored a book entitled Breaking the Chains of Psychological Slavery [2], where he argues that there is a need to become mentally free. His writings suggest that African Americans have been psychologically enslaved and must be proactive in their liberation. The writer understands that the image of African Americans within the church is often limited by collective imagery of the African American racial identity that was formed in part from its struggle and European history of slavery. Akbar argues that to be mentally free, one must be brave and willing to endure loneliness. He writes, "The chains are very heavy and are interconnected, which requires us to free each other as we free ourselves." Like many others who see a difference in Black versus non-Black churches, Dr. Akbar believes that the faith of African Americans must not be one that was used to place and keep Blacks in subjection. Instead, it should be a faith that believes in the right to be free, and like Nat Turner, Harriet Tubman, Sojourner Truth, John Brown, Denmark Vesey, Frederick Douglass, and many other abolitionists, faith must use faith to become free. However, work must go along with faith to promote change in society, the corporate world, and the church. One must stand up for justice, even if standing alone.

Change is never an easy process for individuals or an organization. Accepting change is often the hardest to do. Researcher Michael Fullan in his book, The Six Secrets of Change [29], slated the guru when discussing organizational change. His research examines six ideas that lead to successful change. These six secrets include 1. Care about your employees, 2. Connect peers with purpose, 3. Capacity building prevails, 4. Learning is the work, 5. Transparency rules, and 6. Systems learn. These six areas comprise the entire context of the body of research his book encompasses. From this body of research, the writer can better understand how to foster a change mindset within the ministry context.

The first secret is to care about or love your employees. For the benefit of the writer's project, this may be transliterated to understand and value those working within the ministry context as much as those served by the ministry. The writer has established a relationship with current leaders and has received a credible reference from the senior pastor, who sets the tone and attitude for those who serve him and his vision within this ministry context. Since gaining this trust, the writer is committed to maintaining this trust by working with great intention and integrity as mind shifts are set to become centered on the theme of equality for women in pulpit ministry and pastorates. An investment of time, literature, and common language development is needed for this process to be successful. There is a symbiotic connection between the senior pastor and the clergymen and women who serve him. Therefore, it is critical that the candidate understands this relationship and builds upon it to make change sustainable and real.

As the writer presented speakers and guests who dug deeper into God's word to explain how and why God has included women in all aspects of the ministry, including the pastorate, the writer hoped that the participants would be open to the message of liberation. This would help create a cohesive body of believers so that this change would be safe and supported.

Teaching this truth to the church's layman helps spread the change of thought and helps some accept change more willingly. Similar in goal are the writings captured by Higginbotham's book, Righteous Discontent: The Women's Movement in the Black Baptist Church, 1880-1920, where she recorded the act of three ladies, Maria Stewart, Sojourner Truth, and Jarena Lee, who were "precursors in adopting a scriptural defense of women's rights." According to Higginbotham, "…to stand before an audience of men and women and offer biblical precedents in denunciation of sexism, slavery, the denial of adequate education to Blacks, and other forms of oppression." It is noted that Jarena Lee was the first woman authorized to preach by Richard Allen, founder of the African Methodist Episcopal Church, in 1819. She was part of the Second Great Awakening and was the first African American woman to have an autobiography published in the United States [93]. Maria Stewart was a free-born African American who became a teacher, journalist, lecturer, abolitionist, and women's rights activist. The first known American woman to speak to a mixed audience of men and women,

White and Black, she was also the first African-American woman to make public lectures and lecture about women's rights and make a public anti-slavery speech [52].

Today, this may look like starting from a small intimate setting where only five or six people are teaching to a larger whole group and where several people would be reiterating and teaching the same truth. This new truth may be met with some resistance; however, with the senior pastor's support, many will abandon their caution and risk trusting the church's leadership because of their loyalty to the organization, the pastor, and the leadership team. Hearing the men of the church declare equality for women would hold critical for all the parishioners. Next would be to build capacity within the congregation to share our truth with others with clarity and understanding. This would be through Bible study groups and demonstrated by the inclusion of women in all facets of pulpit ministry.

Finally, all these behaviors would be understood through a social context of rewards and punishments. Rewards are simple acceptances into close fellowship and inner circles, and punishments are the pushbacks and rejection from the political hotspots within and around the ministry context. The writer understands that the backlash could accompany the failure to reach the leadership team and bring about the desired change of mindset and behaviors. Additionally, the risk of being ostracized and characterized as a troublemaker is ever-present. No one wants to be rejected by spiritual leaders, especially not those in one's context. Misjudging the outcomes could jeopardize the relationships developed and credibility earned from the years of service and fellowship within the ministry context. However, the writer considers this risk well worth the effort.

Social Consideration

The writer understands that people at a select Baptist church situated in West Birmingham are varied in age, groups, and interests within the context of this ministry. This ministry context extends itself via social networks and traditional face-to-face meetings. The social construct reflects that of the community it serves and the broader context of the city of Birmingham, Alabama. The candidate understands that the gap among age groups can be reduced with social networking. Further, the writer understands that for this project to galvanize the social support needed to succeed, it must include and interact strategically with various existing groups.

In this ministry context, how women are viewed seems to be part of a "group think" phenomenon among members. The leadership has charismatic and positional authority to influence the thinking and beliefs of its congregants. The candidate does not suggest that something malicious and purposeful is happening; rather, the author believes that it is pass-along teaching that has never been challenged with forward-thinking or the exegesis of God's Word. Many of the congregants have joined this ministry context with the belief that much of what the pastor espouses is in alignment with their own beliefs, and some were born and raised by their parents at this church and have continued to attend. However, a few may have been inspired by the leadership and joined in cosigning with the leader's vision. In turn, the leader may not have purposefully rejected the full inclusion of women in all aspects of ministry or as pastors, but the politics that drive the organization have. The politics are defined by the affiliation of other churches or organizations that are vocal about their belief in limiting women's roles in ministry. This organization subscribes to a body of teaching that flatly rejects the ability of women to ever teach or preach to men or ever pastor a congregation. On one occasion, the candidate was invited to preach at a local convention worship setting but was relegated to a podium at the side of the pulpit. However, the preacher that followed was a male who preached from the pulpit and was not relegated to a podium at the side. Additionally, the male preacher was paid more from a different financial source.

Regardless of the root causes, the problem exists, and social interaction with people who have, for whatever the reason, bought into the belief that this thinking is reflective of their core beliefs or the will of God. This will require the writer to develop relationships and provide solid information that the leadership is willing to accept and refuse to challenge its legitimacy. Relationship building and truth building are the project's foundation for real change to happen and be sustained.

The writer is familiar with different groups within the ministry context and has established credibility in ministry among her leadership team. She has been allowed limited-expression about this topic but has been present at meetings where she noted that a simple task of changing jargon to include the possibility of females in the pastorate was quickly rejected. The singular voice in this context believed that women could teach, but not from the pulpit and not with the same ability as men. This belief was shared between men and women alike.

Understanding the social constructs within the ministry context of A select Baptist church situated West in Birmingham, AL, illuminates and instructs the writer's ministry in many practical ways. One way, in particular, is the way information is disseminated. It is critical that leadership is a part of any needed change. When the senior pastor is supportive, his influence can help persuade others to listen. The senior pastor can directly and positively impact those in his inner circle, including those powers that exist in the political sphere. He can gauge the political thermostat to know when the timing is optimum and when others are willing to invest the effort to re-evaluate belief systems. The writer has come to understand the value of having key leadership support and the wisdom of understanding and taking advantage of timing.

Another practical illumination is the how-to approach to deeply held core beliefs in a group setting. Approaching people about things they hold dear in a group setting can be intimidating and confrontational. The writer has learned that people respond differently in large groups versus small groups or individual settings. Those who lead change must be prayerful, considerate of how change happens, and understand how to allow people time to make adjustments for real, sustainable change.

As a result, this writer invited the leadership teams to strategically design meetings to assess attitudes towards women's equality in pulpit and pastorate ministry via pre-and post-assessments. Each session began by reassuring the participants that our senior pastor had stamped his approval on this study. The writer invited ministers to discuss the Word of God in a small group setting. This approach was less threatening and the least intimidating. Leaders were able to ask questions and were allowed to express thoughts and ideas. This approach lessens the stress and strengthens core beliefs.

The writer understands the importance of confidentiality. Therefore the reporting and interpretation of data are absent information identifying any particular person. However, the writer feels that the life lessons from these sessions brought about change and new realizations. These truths undeniably helped foster a more pliable pathway for larger audiences to digest information and experience such a glorious change.

Current Issues

Recent politics and news flashes have concurrent themes that directly impact the writer and this project. Many of these themes address the role of the woman. They point to women's development and evolutionary process of finding their voice and being recognized in society as equal. Not only do the current trends push forward this project, but they also inform the writer of a broader background that has been the foundational anchor of this project altogether. Because there have been so many different trends, the writer has chosen to categorize them in three different areas: 1. Developing a clear voice, 2. Extending a global cry for change, and 3. Knowing when enough is enough.

First, one major current trend that impacts this research project and sets the context for this project is the "Me-Too" campaign that has become a movement. With a large variety of local and internationally-related names, the movement is one against sexual harassment and sexual assault. The phrase "Me Too" was initially used in this context on social media in 2006, on MySpace, by sexual harassment survivor and activist Tarana Burke. This trend began as a rumble among celebrities that silence was no longer accepted. It started an outrage in a country that was finally ready to hear and respond to women being treated as property or objects rather than intelligent people deserving equal respect as men. It exposed the sexually exploited, behind-the-scenes "good ole boy" culture where women of all colors, shapes, sizes, and social statuses were used and treated as objects of affection. The caveat of their participation was their acceptance. Many knew, but no one was urged to bring about the change needed because the problem was not seen as a problem but rather as a culture.

Several things led to the voice of respect for women. Money, social status, and acceptance were once the protectors of this heinous behavior—even when many whispered about it. It wasn't hidden; it was tolerated until 2017, when a courageous woman spoke out against the abuse and garnered support. The time was right, the opportunity for change had come, and many women began to reveal their hurts and identify their abusers and bring down a long-running wrong as each woman developed a clear voice. Men were also involved in this voice. Soon, the "Me Too" movement became an unstoppable force that intruded the political and celebrity world with a fierce force to affect change. Celebrity after celebrity came forth, and person after person was being fired, discredited, or sued. It was clear that women would no longer allow this behavior to continue. Women had found a clear voice. The most recent awards night was full of women receiving awards and being championed as equal to men to seal this accomplishment. One of the reasons the "Me Too" movement was so timely is the current global cry for change.

In contrast, the 2016 election was much different from any election the writer has ever witnessed or read about. history was rewritten by the crude tactics and mean strategies that played out in the media and worldwide. Never before in a campaign had the world witnessed such divisiveness since the Proclamation Declaration many decades ago. The nation was at war within and against itself. Racism at its worst was seen in its leadership. Women were again referred to as objects by this world leader. This time, the world listened, and many frowned with distaste. Yet, many women supported him as a candidate and ignored all implications that these remarks would prove to be lethal to the success that women and Blacks had gained over the years.

It wasn't long before the world understood that this new leader did not respect women as being equal to men. His selection of staff and remarks on women's bodies confirmed his disdain and disrespect toward most women. He spoke in the ears of the world. Rather than turning a deaf ear, the world revoked the idea as the media tried to hold the world leader accountable for his words. Soon, massive demonstrations and protests led by women began to form and join a resistance movement that the world would participate in efforts to cry for change. The writer believes that this intolerance and world involvement in demanding a change set the stage for the "Me Too" movement to be as effective as it is. This has reignited a conversation about sexual assault with women using the "#Me Too" with activist Tirana Burke, who started the campaign about a decade ago. "Me Too is so powerful because somebody had said it to me, and it changed the trajectory of my healing process," Burke says. Again, celebrities used their platforms to demand respect for women and counter the world leader's ill-spoken words against women.

Even though it is not directly related to my research, it's worth acknowledging the result of the behavior of the previous president and the white nationalist rally in Charlottesville, Virginia in August of 2017. The event painted a grim picture for those who wanted to believe that America had rid herself of racism and that the struggle for equality for all was over. However, the rally was an effort to unite the right-wing and resulted in the loss of life and several injuries. The world noticed the unveiled faces of both young and older men and women, all of whom were White, who rallied to protect the confederate monument.

Many of them had weapons as well as mean chants and slogans. The fight to protect the overthrow of confederate monuments was the catalyst that released the evil that lived in the hearts of those who supported such hatred. Many believe that the president of the free world fueled the energy displayed by his anti-semantic rhetoric and slogan, "Make America Great Again," which is interpreted by many as going back to the slavery or Jim Crow era where Whites were in control of everything. Finally, "enough is enough" speaks to the outbursts of protests against the bigotry and racism that the world leader unleashed through the hate-filled rhetoric he continues to feed his base supporters. Police brutality had increased (or at least the witnessing of police brutality had gained momentum) and was shown from individual smart devices to news outlets worldwide. People had become active in advocacy for fairness for all mankind, especially young Black lives. The Black Lives Matter movement is an example of resistance against the continued police brutality in various states. Several different trends are in this category.

New and reoccurring conflicts were uprising simultaneously on a national scale. Attention to police brutality was increasing. Colin Kaepernick used his voice and lost his career standing up for young Blacks who were systematically targeted by police brutality. Although much attention was given to the Black males, whose lives were taken by police even while in a surrendered unarmed position, Black women were also being affected by police brutality through trauma, pain, and loss of life and loved ones. Riots and protests swarmed the national news as the global group Black Lives Matter responded to the call for justice and liberation for people of color. This group has three major co-founders, all of whom are women, Alicia Garza, Opal Tometi, and Patrisse Cullors, who organize and actively voice, support, and push for justice and equality for Black lives. This group is a nationally recognized organization with grass-root members around the country. Current trends point to breaking silence and the ability to hear the woman's voice. Her voice, once ignored and objectified, now possesses power and persuasiveness. It points to a new era of life where women can be viewed as equal to men. Yet, the struggle continues in efforts to break the systematic policies, procedures, and practices that created the former culture and would otherwise silence women and hold them captive. Jesus, the liberator, has come to set all captives free.

CHAPTER IV

METHODOLOGY

Purpose of this Study and Hypothesis

The context of this study has never had a female pastor, and very few women are ordained as ministers. Also, none can participate in ministry opportunities equal to the male ministers who are members of this church. The purpose of this study is to determine the perceptions of gender equality in church ministry. Specifically, the researcher believes that if the female ministers at Greater Calvary Missionary Baptist Church received training on gender equality in ministry, their knowledge of gender equality would increase. Since the inception of Greater Calvary Missionary Baptist Church – which is the context of the writer's ministry – female preachers have been denied equal opportunities in ministry. While good intention and strong conviction beg to maintain the status quo, change is needed.

Currently, the writer has observed women being denied the equal opportunity to participate in certain duties even if they are ordained, and full inclusion in ministry activities is well-defined and restricted. The influence of culture from African American church history has impacted the progress of women's liberation. Dr. Edward Wimberly [94] explained that behaviors are learned and often passed down from one generation to the next. In his dissertation "Eradicating Gender Bias in Church Leadership [15]," Dr. Ernest Burroughs further states that the church does not look at or view women as they do men for and in leadership, which is a big issue, especially in the Baptist Church. This disproportion of male ordinations versus female ordinations speaks to the accessibility of males to further their ministry as pastors. Most of the males who were a part of the ministry were immediately courted to pastor churches, leaving the female ministers behind. This phenomenon exists beyond the scope of the context of this ministry and extends to related churches, districts, and conventions with similar practices and beliefs.

Data Collection Instrument and the Rationale for the Research Design

This mixed-methods approach utilizes a qualitative case study with semi-structured open-ended interview questions and a quantitative design to analyze descriptive and inferential data. The researcher conducted interviews with participants to explore perceptions of equitable ministry opportunities for women in the context of this study. Case study research involves studying an issue explored through one or more cases within a bounded system. This method was used to describe systematically and accurately the perceptions and experiences reflected by each participant. A case study allows the researcher to use multiple measures of data and methods to investigate profoundly and extend to broader meaning. John Creswell, in his book, Research Design Qualitative & Quantitative Approaches [21], also defined case study as qualitative research where the researcher investigates a case or multiple cases over time through detailed, in-depth data collection involving multiple sources of data. The case study has a long history of use across different disciplines, including anthropology and sociology. The researcher also evaluated quantitative data. Using descriptive and inferential data allows inquiry for a broader perspective of the subject. The researcher used the Statistical Package for the Social Sciences (S.P.S.S.), a tool used to measure statistical data to conduct an ANOVA or a statistical technique used to measure differences among variables.

Research Questions

One central question guides this research: To what extent are female ministers perceived as equal to male ministers? The following are sub-questions that help guide this inquiry. First, how do female ministers compare their opportunities to officiate burials, marriages, baptisms, and other church rites to male ministers within this context? Second, in what ways are female ministers encouraged to preach the gospel compared to the encouragement of male ministers? Third, to what extent do female ministers believe they have equal opportunities to pastor churches compared to opportunities for male ministers to pastor?

Data Collection Procedures

A recorded face-to-face and telephone interview was arranged to conduct a semi-structured open-ended interview. Member checking was encouraged upon transcription of the recorded interview. The researcher also conducted closed-ended surveys to capture descriptive and inferential data with each key ministry participant in this study. With approval granted by the participants, feedback was reviewed, and updates were made as needed. Archived data was reviewed as it related to the inquiry. Data included agendas, minutes from meetings, notes, and memos.

Data Analysis

Matrices were used to display data results. First, for the coding process, all tape-recorded interviews were transcribed; the researcher reviewed all data at least three times before developing categories, themes, and patterns. As patterns emerged from the data, themes were given. Second, responses were sorted and grouped by research questions. A master coding list was completed that included all responses to each question, and a frequency count was then conducted. Third, using the master coding list in step 2, the researcher coded the manuscript of each participant, noting when additional references were made to each response category. The coding list was then finalized. Fourth, the analysis of each response to the research questions and the analysis of each transcript were completed. Fifth, the researcher reviewed all transcripts to confirm major findings, themes, and patterns. Next, the researcher analyzed the quantitative data using S.P.S.S. to measure descriptive data, including frequency, central tendencies, and measures of dispersion and variations. Also, the researcher used data to understand the difference among variables of the study to explore the subject matter further. Finally, a comparison of the findings to the literature was conducted and reported.

Limitations

The most prevailing limitation of this study was the sample size. For this study, one church and its pre-selected group of parishioners and ministers were investigated to understand gender equality in ministry phenomena. The small size of the study participants may have jeopardized the generalization of the study results. Purposive sampling was also a limitation since it lacks wide generalization.

Another limitation is the researcher's bias. The researcher was included in the research reporting because of the qualitative nature of studying phenomena. Inter-rater reliability was established by having an outside reader analyze the data from the study independently and compare the findings. Data collection was limited to interviews, observations, and documents from participants.

Selection of Case

Purposive sampling was used for this mixed-methods research approach to identify the site that would purposely inform the understanding of the phenomena of female ministers' equality in ministry duties. The population for this study included one church and selected members from that church.

Lesson Plans

Lesson 1: "The Biblical Perspective of Gender Difference: Was There Gender Equality when God Created Mankind?" (See Appendix B)

Objectives:

- Participants were able to define "Man" or "Mankind" according to the Bible.
- Participants were able to explain the purpose of humanity according to Genesis.
- Participants were able to discern culture versus Scripture truths.
- Participants were given the definition of gender equality.

Materials/Resources:

- Article by Steve Calagna, "Women in Ministry."
- Book by Katie Canon, Womanism and the Soul of the Black Community.

Scriptures: Genesis 1: 27; Genesis 5:2; Galatians 3:28.

Important Definition:

Gender equality is a set of actions, attitudes, and assumptions that provide opportunities and create expectations about individuals; the process of allocating resources, programs, and decision-making fairly to both males and females without any discrimination on the basis of sex…and addressing any imbalances in benefits available to males and females [66].

Key scripture: Genesis 1: 26-27

> *Then God said, "Let us make mankind in our image, in our likeness, so that they may rule over the fish in the sea and the birds in the sky, over the livestock and all the wild animals, and over all the creatures that move along the ground." So God created mankind in his own image, in the image of God he created them; male and female he created them.*

This text explains that mankind was both male and female and was made in the image and likeness of God. Subtext: Genesis 5:2, male and female created He them. And on the day, they were created, He called them "man" Genesis 5:2 and supporting text: Galatians 3:28. As an introduction to the idea of spiritual equality, these foundational scriptures shaped the understanding of the term "man."

Participants were asked to understand that the term man does not describe domestic roles but rather addresses the nature of creation that separates humanity from other creation. This distinction implies that God did not create an inferior or superior creation by design, although the male was created first and the woman taken from a male's rib. Rather, God created the two to complement for purpose. Phyllis Trible [83] writes: "From the beginning, the word mankind or humankind is synonymous with the phrase "male and female." The parallelism between males and females shows that sexual differentiation does not mean hierarchy but rather equality. Created simultaneously, male and female are not superior and subordinate. Neither has power over the other, in fact, both are given equal power. Male and female were made in the image of God."

Male and female are treated equally, neither given dominion over the other. God does not identify himself with sexuality. Sexual differentiation of humankind is not a description of God. It depicts male and female in freedom and uniqueness and upholds the transcendence of the deity of God [83]. However, the Bible does highlight female and male imagery for God.

Lesson points:

1. God created mankind equally.
2. The term mankind includes both male and female.
3. The fall of mankind in the Hebrew culture became a catalyst for male dominance.

Lesson 2: "The Struggles of Women: Setting the Captives Free."

Objectives:

Participants were able to identify bondages that Jesus addressed in his ministry.

Participants were able to understand gender bias and inequity.

Important Definition:

Gender equality—A set of actions, attitudes, and assumptions that provide opportunities and create expectations about individuals; the process of allocating resources, programs, and decision-making fairly to both males and females without any discrimination on the basis of sex…and addressing any imbalances in benefits available to males and females [66].

Materials/Resources:

Book by Evelyn Brooks Higginbotham, Righteous Discontent, The Women's Movement in the Black Baptist Church, 1880-1920.

Dissertation by Dr. Ernest Burroughs, "Eradicating Gender-Bias in Church Ministry."

Scriptures: Luke 4:18; John 10:10; Numbers 27.

Key scripture: Luke 4:18.

"The Spirit of the Lord is upon me because He has anointed me to preach…"

Subtext: John 10:10, Numbers 27.

This exploration of scripture questions the cultural bondage of mankind and dares to challenge one to explore the question of spiritual inequality between genders as a form of bondage. The daughters of Zelophehad and their request to Moses that they are given their father's inheritance in Numbers 27 will be explored. This lesson will also dive deeply into the text, Righteous Discontent by Evelyn Higginbotham to examine the barriers women have had to face in different facets of leadership, particularly in the church.

Lesson Points:

1. The role of Black females in the collective ethos of racial self-help is significant to enacting change in the lives of all Black people.

2. Eradicating gender bias in church frees women to minister.

3. The Spirit of the Lord empowers women to preach.

Lesson 3: The Ministry Calling of Jesus: "Understanding How Jesus Calls People to Ministry."

Objectives:

Participants were able to understand how women were included in sharing the gospel.

Participants were able to discern culture versus Scripture truths.

Materials/Resources:

Book by Fredrick C. Tiffany and Sharon H. Ringe, Biblical Interpretation: A Roadmap

Book by Wyatt Walker, Somebody's Calling My Name

Book by Phyllis Trible God and the Rhetoric of Sexuality

Scriptures: Mark 16:9; Luke 8:2; Philippians 4:3; Judges 4; Luke 10:1-10.

Key scripture: Mark 16:9.

Mary Magdalene was the one first to witness Jesus' resurrection and was given the charge to go and tell others.

Subtext: Luke 8:2.

Mary Magdalene was one of the ones who accompanied Jesus, and some have referred to her as equal to the apostles. She was also one of many women who ministered to and with Jesus and have directly benefited from the ministry of Jesus. Paul urges others to care for the females who "co-labored" in the gospel with him in Philippians 4:3. God calls to Deborah in the Old Testament, Book of Judges. Women were among the seventy-two sent out, Luke 10:1-11.

Lesson Points:

1. Women were included in the sharing of the gospel.

2. The call to ministry is unique to the will and purposes of God, not

man.

3. The call of ministry is heard through various circumstances and situations.

Lesson 4: "Vessels and Gifts of the Holy Spirit, Pt. 1".

Objectives:

Participants were able to identify vessels of the Holy Spirit according to Scripture.

Participants were able to discern culture versus Scripture truths.

Materials/Resources:

Book by Andrew Billingsley, Mighty Like a River.

Book by Ella Mitchell, Women to Preach.

Book by Rosetta Ross, Witnesses.

Scriptures: 2 Timothy 2:21; Galatians 3:28.

Key scripture: 1 Corinthians 12:4-11.

Subtext: Ephesians 4:11-16.

These texts were used to help participants reframe ideas of how the Holy Spirit ministers and through whom the Holy Spirit may minister. This lends itself to understanding that it is indeed the Holy Spirit who ministers through humanity and not vice versa which expands the ministry of the Holy Spirit to whosoever is yielded and obedient.

Lesson Points:

1. There are a variety of spiritual gifts which are given by God's Holy Spirit.

2. The gifts of the Holy Spirit are not bound by gender.

3. The gifts of the Holy Spirit make us one.

Lesson 5: "Vessels and Gifts of the Holy Spirit, Pt .2."

Objectives:

Participants were able to understand the function of the Holy Spirit and its impact on the ministry and the expansion of inclusion of women in ministry.

Participants were able to identify various spiritual gifts.

Materials/Resources:

Book by Charles Bryant, Rediscovering our Spiritual Gifts: Building Up the Body of Christ Through the Gifts of the Spirit.

Book by Kenneth Copeland, The Woman Question.

Book by Ella Mitchell, Women to Preach.

S.H.A.P.E. a gift assessment tool

Scripture: Luke 8:1-3; Acts 16:11-15; Romans 16:7.

Key scripture: 2 Timothy 2:21.

Subtext: Galatians 3:28.

These texts were used to help participants reframe ideas of how the Holy Spirit ministers and through whom the Holy Spirit may minister. The assessment tool gave participants a way to discover their Spiritual gift sets.

Lesson Points:

1. Gifts of the Spirit are equally given to men and women.

2. God used women in leadership.

3. Women of the early church operate in spiritual gifts as they do today.

Lesson 6: "The Great Commission."

Objective:

Participants were able to identify the "Great Commission" and recognize its issuance is inclusive according to Scripture.

Participants were able to discern cultural versus Scriptural truths and the New Testament practices.

Materials/Resources:

Book by Richard Davidson, Women in Ministry.

Book by Rosetta Ross, Witnesses.

Book by Ella Mitchell, Women to Preach.

Scriptures: Matthew 28:19-20.

Key scripture: Matthew 28:19-20.

The commission given from Jesus to Believers is to expand the Kingdom of God through teaching, discipleship, and baptism. This commission is not aimed at a particular gender, but it includes all people. This lesson compelled listeners to consider how the customs of the Old Testament shape our beliefs in women's roles and responsibilities in the Kingdom of God compared to New Testament practices.

Lesson Points:

1. Women were included in the Great Commission.

2. Women are empowered by the Spirit of God.

3. Women had a significant role in the growth of the church.

The lesson plans for this model were carefully constructed and considered to ensure that each training session built upon the previous one. The researcher understands that retention for adults requires repetition and connection. Also, to add value to each session, the research matched the lesson to the expertise and interest of each facilitator. The facilitators offered an extensive background in their subject matter and delivered the information in a manner so that listeners could comprehend and extend their understanding. Each lesson had a pointed goal or objective, and pre-discussed questions were purposefully designed to engage the listener and help the facilitators fulfill the expectation of teaching for their sessions. These efforts combined helped participants to maximize their benefit from the study. Each lesson sought to reinforce the previous lessons with a creative question and answer method.

CHAPTER V

FIELD EXPERIENCE

Timeline Review

On July 6, 2019, the researcher hosted the orientation of her project in the Fellowship Hall of Greater Calvary Missionary Baptist Church with selected female ministers and laypersons to discuss the study and the timeline. This orientation included discussion regarding the consent form and appointments for individual interviews. The researcher utilized a committee of people to orchestrate a sign-in process to help transition the potential participants from one station to the next. First, attendees were asked to sign in with their names and contact information. The attendees were given consent forms and time to review them individually at another station. Next, the researcher moved them to a third station, as a whole group, to read each item of the consent agreement with all participants prior to signing the agreement. At which time, a space was given for questions. Since none were raised, all attendees were asked to sign the form if they were willing to participate. The forms were then collected, and the researcher completed a check-off list to indicate the process through which potential candidates needed to be oriented to the study before the first class. After the checklist was completed, participants were given the pre-test.

In addition to reviewing the consent form, expectations were discussed, social norms were established, and light refreshments were served. During the hour-long orientation, participants communicated interest and commitment. A total of twenty-five women were invited to participate; however, only six women were present and participated in the orientation. Due to a holiday and a schedule conflict for many potential participants, a second orientation was scheduled for July 13, 2019, before the first lesson.

On July 13, 2019, the second orientation was scheduled at the same time and location. The researcher invited forty women to participate; however, thirty-two women and five men participated. Again, the researcher discussed expectations, established social norms, and scheduled appointments for individual interviews. Twenty-six consent forms were collected, and an expression of understanding and willingness to participate was noted. (Appendix A) The researcher reminded all individuals of their right to withdraw from the study and how the information would be handled before, during, and after the study. Immediately following this orientation, the pre-test was given to those who were not present at the initial orientation (twenty-six individuals). (Appendix D) The researcher hired a vendor to provide refreshments.

During the orientation, the student and her contextual associates maintained sign-in sheets (Appendix F), documentation of completed consent forms (checklist), a calendar of events, and materials for participants to take notes. In addition, the researcher gifted each participant with a journal and a pen in appreciation for their participation. All participants were Greater Calvary Missionary Baptist Church Birmingham members except for two guests who served on the researcher's committee.

Dr. Tommie L. Lewis, the Senior Pastor of Bethel Baptist, Pratt City, was in attendance and greeted the facilitator, Dr. James Coleman, and the participants and assured them that he was in total agreement with the proposed study.

Training Session/Classes

Session 2, Lesson I

We began our training sessions on July 13, 2019, at 11:30 AM. The facilitator for the session was Dr. James E. Coleman, Jr. D. Min., Director, Doctor of Ministry Program (Virginia University of Lynchburg). His lesson topic was "The Biblical Perspective of Gender

Difference: Was There Gender Equality When God Created Mankind?" The agenda for this lesson was as follows: 11:30 AM – introduction of guest lecturer; 11:35–11:40 AM – prayer and blessing of food (pre-test for new participants); 11:40 AM-12:00 PM – Lunch; 12:00–1:00 PM – lessons. (Appendix E)

At this session, thirty-seven people were in attendance consisting of males and females, laypersons and ministers. Each person consented to participate in the study and seemed eager to hear the lesson. Dr. Coleman provided supplemental materials and guided notes for his presentation. The guiding questions were: Did the creation of man include all humanity or only males? Were males and females created equally? Is the "Fall" and Hebrew culture seen as the catalyst for male dominance? Dr. Coleman opened his lesson with one written message and a picture to reinforce it. He wrote the following:

Your situation and your location are never the basis for your identification.

A. Identification is rooted in your creation, not your location.

B. Never allow where you are in life to define who you are.

C. When you know location or situation does not define your identification, no location can place a premature limitation on your destination.

D. Identification is in your creation.

E. Discover your creation-discover your destiny.

(Dr. Coleman, Presentation, July 13, 2019) [19].

Upon sharing these statements, the audience began to yell, "Teach us, Teach us!" Dr. Coleman continued his lesson by driving home the idea of theology versus "snakeology" among similar themes to point to the original intent of God's creation prior to the fall of mankind. He emphasized that the dominance of men over women

> Dr. Coleman emphasized that the dominance of men over women was not the design of God but of a snake.

was not the design of God but of a snake. Supplemental material provided included a picture, lyrics to a song, and an excerpt from the reading, which further pointed to the idea that cultural truths and spiritual truths do not always align, specifically regarding race, gender and politics. Hierarchy and separation have been supported and even inflamed by cultural idealism regarding race, gender, and politics in the name of religion. Hence, equality was the intent of God from the beginning, and God created the two to complement each other for a purpose.

Additionally, Dr. Coleman noted Genesis 1:26-28, " God said, "Let us make man in our image, in our likeness," and Genesis 5:2, "He created them male and female and blessed them." There are two accounts of the creation, and from the beginning, God intended that men and women were created equal. Dr. Coleman asked the question, "Do you have the courage and commitment to be honest about what has been done in the name of Christ?"

Dr. Coleman continued to exegete 1 Corinthians 11 to remind us that Paul said that women could lead prayer and prophesy or declare the Word of God in Church as long as they do it under the cultural display of submitting to the elders of the church and their husbands. So, Paul cannot mean without equivocation that women must be silent in the church. The church failed in fighting against the brutal oppression of women. We see in the Corinthian church that the gospel came into this fallen world and reclaimed equality for women when injustice and the curse of sin had taken it away [6]. God created us, male and female, with distinctions in how we are meant to operate in this world and with each other. We see the man as independent and the woman as a dependent. Sin distorted and exaggerated the way that God designed us by turning men's independence into tyranny and dominance over women. Sin came into the world and changed everything.

The gospel was needed and came and spoke to the inequality and to teach men how to lead properly in servanthood and humility, not dominance. Dr. Coleman explained to the class that the "gospel came and destroyed all of the wrong distinctions in gender created by sin."

He further talked about hierarchy, the system in which people or things are arranged according to their importance. Hierarchy destroys the world based on race, class, and gender, and it also suggests that certain people do not matter because God is endorsing such notions of inequality and inequity. The naïve assumption is that some people are ignorant or unequipped to function at certain levels based on race, class, or gender.

Dr. Coleman quoted Dr. Zelda Kitt when she said, "it is not about the body or gender of the body, it is about the work and the quality of the surrendered vessel to God the Creator." He left us with Galatians 3:28; There is neither Jew nor Greek, there is neither bond nor free, there is neither male nor female: for ye are all one in Christ Jesus.

Finally, Dr. Coleman's handout on Men, Women, and Biblical Equality informed the participants that the Bible teaches the full equality of men and women in the creation and redemption, and at Pentecost, the Holy Spirit came upon men and women alike.

Session 3, Lesson II

On July 20, 2019, Rev. Geraldine Moore, M.R.E., the candidate's contextual associate, facilitated the second lesson. The lesson's topic was "The Struggles of Women: Setting the Captives Free." The agenda for this lesson was as follows: 11:30 AM – introduction of guest lecturer; 11:35–11:40 AM – prayer and blessing of food; 11:40 AM-1200 P.M. – Lunch; 12:00–1:00 PM – lesson.

During this lesson, Rev. Moore shared handouts on different types of bias and ways to identify and overcome bias. There were 29 participants present, including men and women. The audience watched a short video during this lesson and was asked to analyze it. The participants discovered that each had some form of bias, and because of the taught bias, we are trained to frame what we see through those lenses. People have both unconscious bias and implicit bias.

Participants were provided a handout to supplement the lesson. Rev. Moore began the conversation with a discussion about Righteous Discontent: The Women's Movement in the Black Baptist Church 1880-1920 by Evelyn Brooks Higginbotham. This discussion also included Eradicating Gender Bias in Church Leadership by Dr. Ernest Burroughs. Rev. Moore addressed gender bias, stereotyping, areas of struggle for women, including economics, violence against women, laws that protected women, and a timeline of women's history. She also provided a list of women in the Bible and their roles and contributions. She spoke of Phoebe as a deacon in Roman 16, about Priscilla in Act 18, Shiphrah and Puah midwives who feared God and saved Moses. She also explained about additional women in the Bible.

- Tamar, daughter-in-law of Judah (Exodus 1)
- Rahab, a prostitute in Jericho (Genesis 38)
- The five daughters of Zelophehad (sisters that went to Moses about their father's inheritance)
- Jehosheba, the aunt of Joash, saved him from death so that David's lineage would continue
- Huldah (2 Kings 22), a prophetess who was married but a prophetess in her own right used by God to declare that the writing found in the temple was authentic

- Lydia (Acts 16 and history as recorded by Josephus) was a businesswoman who was one of the first converts to Christianity

- Priscilla (Romans 16), who was married to Aquila, traveled with Paul, described as "fellow workers in Christ Jesus."

- The women who witnessed the resurrection of Christ in Matthew 28.

Along with her lesson, she provided guided notes for participants. The three guiding questions were: How does Jesus embrace the role of women? What is the significance of including the actions of women in the Bible? Does eradicating gender bias in church free women to minister [63]?

Rev. Moore reminded the class that leadership was nothing new to women. She mentioned Cleopatra, Queen Elizabeth, women who led in the abolition of slavery like Harriet Tubman, Sojourner Truth, and others, and people who led in the Civil Rights movement like Mrs. Rosa Parks, Mrs. Coretta Scott King, and others. She also spoke of C.E.O.s of Fortune 500 companies, women who served in cabinet-level positions; and women like Bishop Vashti McKenzie, Rabbi Sally Jane Priesand, Pastor Amy Butler, the first woman pastor of The Riverside Church; and Rabi' A. Keeble and M. Hasna Maznavi founders of the first two female-run mosques in the country. Women are indeed leaders.

Rev. Moore also discussed the book "Righteous Discontent, The Women's Movement in the Black Baptist Church, 1880-1920" by

Evelyn Brooks Higginbotham. This book aimed to create a forum through which Black people could voice their spiritual, economic, political, and social concerns. Blacks were denied access to public places; the church functioned as a critical arena where issues were aired, even though women often took the back seat to men even though they were both equally oppressed.

Session 4, Lesson III

On July 27, 2019, Pastor Tyree Anderson, D. Min. presented the lesson entitled, "The Ministry Calling of Jesus: Understanding How Jesus Calls People to Ministry." The agenda for this lesson was as follows: 11:30 AM – introduction of guest lecturer; 11:35-11:40 AM – prayer and blessing of food; 11:40-12:00 PM – Lunch; 12:00-1:00 PM – presentation of the lesson.

During Dr. Anderson's presentation, three points were expressly stressed: The call to "ministry" or "preaching" is not limited by gender women were included in the sharing of the gospel. God alone determines the will and purpose of the call. Every call is unique circumstances, and situations vary on when, where, and how the call is heard. Twenty-three participants were in attendance, and of the twenty-three, twenty were females.

Dr. Anderson quoted Dr. Peter Wherry, a former Virginia Union University professor and current pastor of the Mayfield Baptist Church, Charlotte, NC, saying, "...all believers are called to preach, but not all are called to pulpit ministry [6]." Dr. Anderson said that the resurrection of Jesus and the commission to "go tell" were given to the women and not to the disciples. He listed the qualifications for one to be an apostle, and looking at the qualifications, the anatomical makeup is not relevant. Dr. Anderson proceeded to quote from Dr. William H. Myers' book God's Yes is Louder than My No: Rethinking the African Call to Ministry and the Irresistible Urge to

> "One of the most divisive matters facing Black churches in our time focused on the hermeneutical issue of the call to ministry, especially the role and function of women in leadership positions in the church."

Preach: A Collection of African American "Call" to ministry and the "Call" Stories [64].

"One of the most divisive matters facing Black churches in our time focused on the hermeneutical issue of the call to ministry, especially the role and function of women in leadership positions in the church." Dr. Anderson noted that the Bible is the chief battleground where this war is waged. Opponents come fully armed with their favorite proof text, sometimes the same text, to battle over who has the right to speak for God. "Yet, I propose to you that the call to ministry or the call to preaching is not a gender debate. Since the resurrection of Jesus, women have been preaching, and I would even go so far as to say that women were the first of the apostles." Dr. Anderson said. Mark 16:9 reveals that Jesus' first appearance was to a woman named Mary Magdalene. Then John 20:11-19 would indicate that Mary Magdalene was an apostle based on these qualifications. Dr. Anderson further stated that Jesus sent the 12 disciples, but it was the women who walked with Him. Those women were his disciples, and Luke names a few, like Joanna, the wife of Herod's steward Chuza, Susann, and many others. (Luke 8: 2-3).

This uniqueness means that God shows no respect for gender; moreover, God alone determines the will and purpose of the call. Dr. Vashti McKenzie, in her book, Not Without a Struggle: Leadership Development for African American Women in Ministry [59], quotes the researcher's fellow hometown scholar, Dr. Cain Hope Felder, an American Biblical scholar, saying, "African American scholars must challenge the Eurocentric mindset for the sake of healthy scholarship and the African American community." Women in the plan of God have always had a leading role. Deborah was a prophet and a judge. Naomi's will and purpose would lead to the eventual coming of the ultimate salvation plan.

According to Dr. Anderson, each person that God calls has a unique calling. Some calls are subtle, and others are elaborate, but each called person has a call story. Dr. Katie Cannon, the founder and establisher of Womanist Theology pens, "women have to reclaim their right to read and interpret sacred texts for themselves and should not have to be subject to the misogynistic patriarchal interest of powerful male readers, and women of color have to insist upon their right to read and interpret the sacred texts for themselves; and should not have to defend or apologize for their interpretations to privileged women in the culture who remain ignorant to how class, race, and colonialism shape and divides us as women." They should not have to re-read the Bible for liberation [18].

Dr. Cannon said that "it is important for women who have been called to ministry or called to preach must remain unique in their calling and not attempt to imitate their male counterparts." Dr. Anderson explained to the participants what the call to ministry or call to preach is not: 1) The Call to "ministry or "preaching is not limited by gender (women were included in sharing of the gospel). 2) God alone determines the will and purpose of the call. And 3) Every call is unique; however, circumstances and situations vary on when, where, and how the call is heard.

In his wrap-up, Dr. Anderson answered various questions from participants concerning women in ministry. He gave the class his contact numbers if they should have additional questions after the session's conclusion. He reminded the class that as men and women of color, we have been disenfranchised and disinherited both in the culture and church. He truly does have a passion for God's Word and God's people.

Session 5, Lesson IV

On August 3, 2019, Dr. Zelda Kitt presented a lesson entitled "Vessels and the Gifts of the Holy Spirit: Part I." The agenda for this lesson was as follows: 11:30 AM – introduction of guest lecturer;

11:35–11:40 AM – prayer and blessing of food; 11:40 AM -12:00 PM – Lunch; 1200-1:00 P.M. – presentation of the lesson. Twenty-seven participants were present for this lesson, three of whom were male attendees.

In this class, Dr. Kitt focused on the vessels of the Holy Spirit. She used handouts and a visual demonstration to lead the discussion about vessels and the Holy Spirit. In addition, she introduced a gift assessment called S.H.A.P.E. to describe and discuss spiritual gifts. S.H.A.P.E. is an acronym that means A) Spiritual Gifts, B) Heart, C) Abilities, D) Personality, and C) Experience. See Appendix D. This resource is an excerpt from a workbook that offers an assessment for people to discover their gifts.

As a visual demonstration, Dr. Kitt placed three cups on the table and poured water into each. Each cup had a different colored substance representing a different lens through which the water interacted. She announced that while the Holy Spirit is pure, He is filtered through earthen vessels, which may interpret or interact differently.

Gifts of the Holy Spirit are God-based, not gender-based. God's plan is inclusive. She reminded the class of Joel 2:28, "and afterward, I will pour out my spirit on all people. Your sons and daughters shall prophesy." Every believer has a gift from God, and the Holy Spirit distributes the gifts as He sees fit [50]. The participants responded to this teaching by requesting additional information and expressing a desire to learn more about their specific gifts.

Dr. Kitt expounded upon Genesis 5:2, where the text says that he created man and blessed them and called their name Adam in the day when they were created, noting God's original intent. Genesis 1:26-27 also says,

Then God said, "Let us make man in our image, in our likeness, and let them rule over the fish of the sea and the birds of the air, over the livestock, over all the earth, and over all the creatures that move along the ground," So God created man in His own image, in the image of God He created him, male and female He created them.

Session 6, Lesson V

On August 10, 2019, Dr. Zelda Kitt presented Part II of "Vessels and Gifts of the Holy Spirit:" The agenda for this lesson was as follows: 11:30 AM introduction of guest lecturer; 11:35–11:40 AM – prayer and blessing of food; 11:40 AM-12:00 PM – Lunch; 12:00–1:00 PM – presentation of the lesson.

During this second class on the Gifts of the Holy Spirit, Dr. Kitt focused primarily on why and to whom gifting is given. The presenter provided additional handouts and made connections to previous lessons. She emphasized the following items: The impact of cultural beliefs about creation, spiritual gifts and callings, leadership gifts, and services gifts. She also provided a diagnostic for interested participants to help guide their understanding of their gift. The attendees expressed interest. Many were recording and writing notes.

Twenty-three participants were present for this class, including four male attendees.

Dr. Kitt's guiding questions were Do the gifts of the Holy Spirit impact ministry selection and calling, and Does God use women in leadership? She told the participants that the gifts of the Holy Spirit are not bound by gender and that the gifts are designed to make us one. She reminded the class of the Biblical account in 1 Corinthians 12:4-11 that there are different kinds of gifts, but the same Spirit distributes them all just as He determines. Dr. Kitt admonished the participants to "stay humble, pray and wait on God to guide them concerning their gifts."

Session 7, Lesson VI

On August 17, the researcher presented the last lesson entitled, "The Great Commission." The researcher supplemented the lesson with handouts and guided questions. The agenda for this lesson was as follows: 11:30 AM – introduction of guest lecturer; 11:35–11:40 AM – prayer and blessing of food; 11:40 AM-12:00 PM – Lunch; 12:00–1:00 PM – lesson. There were thirty participants for this lesson.

The presenter provided additional handouts, as noted in Appendix B, and emphasized the following items: The impact of culture and beliefs about creation, inclusiveness of women, biblical support for women in ministry and leadership roles, and that the commandment "to go" is for all people that included women. She reminded the class that the book of Genesis records two accounts of the creation of man and that in neither account was one created inferior or superior. The fall of mankind in the Hebrew culture became a catalyst for male dominance. It was the curse of the Fall that hierarchy was established. Dr. James Coleman, Jr. called this "snake talk." God created mankind equally.

The presenter referenced lesson two from Evelyn Higginbotham's book, Righteous Discontent, which examined the barriers women faced in different facets of leadership, particularly in the church. In addition, she also restated that the gifts of the Holy Spirit are not bound by gender, and the call to ministry is unique to the will and purpose of God, not man. The Holy Spirit uses whoever is yielded and obedient; God calls who God chooses. Several examples of women being called and used by God in His plan for mankind were discussed.

The facilitator further emphasized the impact of culture and certain religious beliefs about creation to be a hindrance to women in ministry and do not understand that the command, in Matthew 28:19, to go and make disciples of all nations is all-inclusive. The researcher gave the participants a fill-in-the-blanks worksheet and allowed them time to work together and complete the test. The participants were then encouraged to answer the questions on a volunteer basis. This was not an in-depth review but a fun activity and a learning and reinforcement tool to recap the five previous lessons.

Session 8, Post-Test, Dinner, and Graduation

103

The agenda for this last session was as follows: 11:30 AM-11:35 – introductions and appreciation from the candidate 11:35 AM-12:05 PM – the post-test was administered, and an extended question and answer session was held with Dr. Zelda Kitt; 12:05–12:45 PM – prayer, blessing of the food and Lunch; 12:45-1:00 P. M. – Graduation, which included the presentation of certificates and letters of appreciation to thirty attendees and participants. See Appendix G and H.

Several attendees participated in the question-and-answer session with Dr. Kitt. Questions were asked about the use of spiritual gifts. For example, one attendee asked, "What do you suggest when you know you have a gift, but it isn't recognized in the church?" Another asked about prophesying and speaking in tongues. Dr. Kitt addressed each question with reference to scripture. Candidate McDonald was asked to expound on the doctoral process and what is next for her in this process. Candidate McDonald now hopes to start a dialogue and training sessions with the associate ministers at Bethel and the surrounding area. During her interview, Dr. Natalie Houghtby-Haddon's suggestion to the candidate was that there needs to be a support group formed that can empower the female preachers, a "safe place" so that they may share their stories. The ministers can encourage each other when it seems as if they are on this journey alone. The candidate also expressed appreciation to all participants for their time and sacrifice. She also expressed her feelings about the sessions. She knows perhaps that she gained as much or more from the sessions than the other participants. She has grown in knowledge and in her resolve to do whatever it takes to make a difference in both Bethel and the ecclesia as a whole.

Conclusion

This phase of the researcher's journey proved incredibly significant. It informed the researcher of the different beliefs shared within the context, and it also provided some insight into how and why people believe as they do. The structure of the study extended beyond the academic structure and served as a catalyst for change within the context of the study. Many participants began to form relationships with some of the presenters and requested that the presenters return to continue teaching on various topics.

The candidate believes that the most profound experience of the study was the willingness of the participants to dig deep and open their minds to the teachings. During each instructional session, the attendees verbally expressed interest and delight. Many were recording using social media, and some even asked for recorded sessions for personal use. Although the study focused primarily on the women, men were also in attendance at each session. The men who attended expressed interest and willingness to participate, which was a plus to the project.

Before the actual study, the presenter experienced nervousness about attendance; however, the presenter found that attendance was no longer an issue once the sessions began. The attendees expressed a desire for ongoing teachings.

The candidate hopes that the readers will be able to use the timeline review to find that this study was implemented with integrity and that she took great strides to ensure voices were heard and acknowledged as the independent examiner sought to determine the merits of the hypothesis.

Results of the Model

The researcher used a mixed-methods approach to collect, analyze and report the results of this study. The hypothesis is that if the female ministers at Greater Calvary Missionary Baptist Church receive training on gender equality in ministry, their knowledge of gender equality will increase. Thirty participants completed the pre/post-test in the quantitative analysis; there were twenty-two participants participated in the qualitative component.

The researcher used S.P.S.S. to conduct a paired T-test to explore the pre/post-test data in the quantitative section. Also, an ANOVA and an Independent T-test were run to analyze demographic data. These reports and graphs show how and where the participants' perceptions differ in five categories: 1. Sex, 2. Age, 3. Education, 4. Leadership Capacity within the church, and 5. Status of Ministry Recognition (license/ordination status). See Appendix C (quantitative instrument).

In the qualitative section, the researcher used coding to identify and report themes from the data provided by the twenty-two participants. Each person was asked five open-ended, semi-structured questions via tape recorder and later transcribed. Member checking for accuracy was allowed for each participant. The guiding question for this research was as follows: To what extent are female ministers perceived as equal to male ministers? Sub-questions included the following: 1. Do you believe that there was gender equality when God created mankind? Please explain. 2. How does Jesus call people to ministry? 3. How significant is self-help in eradicating gender bias? 4. How do gifts of the Holy Spirit make us one? And 5. How were women included in the "Great Commission?" See Appendix B (qualitative instrument).

Quantitative Results

Thirty participants completed the study. They completed a pre-test of six demographic questions and 21 quantitative questions using a 1-5 Likert scale, a rating scale used to measure attitudes or opinions. With this scale, respondents were asked to rate items on a level of agreement [78]. Participants then attended six lessons based on several topics regarding the evidence and benefit of women in ministry. After attending the lessons, participants received a post-test survey which contained the same questions as the pre-test.

Of the thirty participants, the demographic information reveals that twenty-four were female participants, and six were male participants. See the graph in Appendix C titled, Sex and Demographics. Of the 30 participants, one completed high school, eleven completed some college, and eighteen obtained a college degree. See the graph in Appendix C titled Education and Demographics. Of the thirty participants, three were between ages forty and forty-nine, five were between ages fifty and fifty-nine, twelve reported being between sixty and sixty-nine, and ten were between ages seventy and seventy-nine. See the graph in Appendix C titled Age Demographics. Of the thirty participants, five identified as laity or members, seventeen identified as part of leadership, seven identified as ministers, and one identified as pastor. Appendix C, titled Main Capacity within the Church Demographics. Of the thirty participants, eighteen reported none licensed, and twelve reported as licensed. See the graph in Appendix C, titled, License Status Demographics. Of the thirty participants, twenty reported not being ordained, and ten reported being ordained (one a minister, and the others are deacons). See the graph in Appendix C, titled, Ordained Status Demographics.

After running a Paired Sample T-Test on all pre-test and post-test questions, including the collective means of all pre-test and post-test questions, Question 15 (God created males and females equally) had the most statistically significant result (p=0.028). A paired T-test is used to measure the statistical significance of a group or population before and after, such as with the pre-and post-test results. For Question 15, the pre-test means (4.4667) minus the post-test mean (4.9333) equaled -0.4667, meaning the post-test scores were higher than the pre-test scores by a statistically significant amount. Isolating female participants resulted in a significance level closer to 0.05 for the cumulative test (Paired Samples; p=0.059). However, Question 20 (Woman played a significant role in the growth of the early church) and question 16 (Male dominance in the Bible is a result of the fall of mankind and Hebrew culture) also showed statistical significance when isolating females (Paired Samples; p=0.027, p=0.020). All three questions featured an increase in post-test scores with respective mean differences of -0.63636 and -0.59051, and - 0.53203. For Question 15, ratings of five increased from 13 to 21. For Question 20, ratings of five increased from 15 to 22, and for Question 16, rating from 21 to 29. See graph 7 in Appendix C, titled Comparisons of Pre-Test and Post Scores for Questions 1-21. The researcher employed the ANOVA test to determine differences among the various groups and found no statistical significance overall—which yielded a null hypothesis; however, it was noted that there was a statistically significant difference for questions 15, 16, and 20. (See depiction on graph 7, titled Comparisons of pre-test and post-test scores for questions 1-21).

Although the post-test scores were higher than the pre-test scores, showing a positive change in opinion toward female church leadership, there was not a statistically significant increase in opinion (Paired Samples Test; p=0.107). See graph 8 in Appendix C, titled, Comparison of Cumulative pre-test and post-test means.

ANOVA and Independent T-Tests were also run to compare the demographic groups within the study in terms of statistically different responses to questions.

There were no statistically significant results for analyses on pre-post test question means for age groups, but one question, Question 11 ("There are examples of women leadership in the Bible"), approached significance (p=0.060). After running a Tukey HSD Multiple Comparisons Test, the age ranges of 70-79 and 40-49, the eldest and youngest participant groups, respectively, showed the closest difference in mean (p=0.080).

Although there was no change in the mean of groups 50-59 and 60-69 (mean rating of 5), 40-49-year-old participants experienced a decrease in favorable ratings towards biblical examples of women leadership, while 70-79-year-old participants experienced an increase in favorable ratings. See graph 9 in Appendix C, titled, Differences Based on Age for Question 11.

Although not significant, there was an increase in acceptance towards women in ministry as age increased. See graph 10 in Appendix C, titled Cumulative Comparison of Average Post Test/Pre-Test Difference Based on age.

Although there were no significant findings for sex, females did show a higher difference in pre-test and post-test scores, while males showed regression in scores (p=0.141). Questions 7 (Men and women are equal in ministry.), 19 (Women of the early church operated in spiritual gifts as women do today.), and 20 (Woman played a significant role in the growth of the early church.) came closest to statistical significance (Independent T-Test; p=0.083, p=0.074, 0.070). Ladies' post-test scores were slightly greater than pre-test scores. Male post-test scores were slightly less than pre-test scores. Females showed more progress than males, but not enough to be statistically significant (Independent T; p=0.141). See graph 11 in Appendix C, titled, Cumulative Comparison of Average Post Test/Pre-Test Difference Based on Sex. Although there was no significant difference for capacity within the church, Question 7 (Men and women are equal in ministry.) and Question 8 (Women face more challenges in ministry than men.) initially showed statistical significance; however, due to few pastoral participants, the Tukey Test [78] showed no statistical significance between any variables.

The Tukey Test, also called Tukey's Honest Significant Difference test, is a post-hoc test based on the standardized range distribution. An ANOVA test can tell you if your results are significant overall, but it will not tell you exactly where those differences lie.

Education

There were no significant differences between means based on educational level, but Question 11 (There are examples of woman leadership in the Bible.) approached significance ($p=0.054$).

Licensing and Ordaining Status

Neither licensing status nor ordaining status within the church showed significance, but the Independent T-Test result for ordaining status was small ($p=0.069$). There were few statistically significant values after analyzing the data. Cumulative analyses showed no significant differences in pre-test and post-test scores, with only a few significant values when isolating for questions about sex. Therefore, based on the candidate's research, the hypothesis -- if the female ministers at Greater Calvary Missionary Baptist Church receive training on gender equality in ministry, then their knowledge of gender equality would increase -- the overall hypothesis is null.

111

Qualitative Results

The researcher conducted a mixed-methods approach which included semi-structured, open-ended interviews within the context of this study. This section aims to report the various themes from thick, rich qualitative data. That is to take the data collected and give a detailed interpretation of the data observed during the project [75]. The study's hypothesis is that if female ministers at Greater Calvary Missionary Baptist Church receive training on gender equality in ministry, their knowledge of gender equality will increase. The guiding question for this research was: To what extent are female ministers perceived as equal to male ministers? Sub-questions include the following: 1. Do you believe that there was gender equality when God created mankind? Please explain. 2. How does Jesus call people to ministry? 3. How significant is self-help in eradicating gender bias? 4. How do gifts of the Holy Spirit make us one? And 5. How are women included in the "Great Commission?"

In this section, the researcher will report findings on each sub-questions that helped understand and answer the guiding question.

Sub-question 1: Do you believe that there was gender equality when God created mankind? Please explain.

The researcher asked this question of twenty-two participants, all females. While each participant stated that there was gender equality when God created males and females, the explanations varied and, to some extent, contradicted what they said. Nineteen of the twenty-two participants talked about the chronological order in which creation is recorded in the Bible, according to Genesis. They each expressed that because of the order in which God created mankind, the order of creation indicated that man was made first and is, to some extent, evidence that God's intent for man to be over the woman. Respondent C concluded,

"If God wanted man and woman to be equal, He would have made them both the same way and at the same time. It shows that God has a divine order and man is to lead. When man sinned, God questioned Adam first. It was Adam who tried to blame Eve."

Respondent B offered, "God hierarchy is the Trinity, man, woman and then children. This is just the way it is."

Respondent H concluded: "Adam was made for God, and Eve was made for Adam. That's God's divine order. If a man finds a woman, not if a woman finds a man. God put man in charge."

Other respondents expressed similar beliefs that the order of the household, both domestically and otherwise, is revealed in Genesis because of the order in which God created mankind. The four who disagreed with this belief talked about the meaning of Adam, citing that God created mankind equally, but after the Fall, man and woman were punished, and one of those punishments was for the woman to answer to the man. Respondent A clearly stated, "God made all of mankind equal from the beginning. When He spoke to Adam, He was speaking to mankind, not a specific person. Respondent A stated,

"Adam means man."

Sub-question 2: How does Jesus call people into ministry?

Of the twenty-two participants, six participants explained that Jesus calls people into ministry through the Word of God; ten participants described that the way Jesus calls people into ministry is by the Holy Spirit; five participants suggested that Jesus calls people into ministry according to the desires or passions that people have, and one participant stated that she was unsure. The dominant themes that emerged were the Word of God establishes the calling and the Holy Spirit does the calling.

The Word of God is referred to as the Holy Scriptures, both Old and New Testaments. The respondents expressed that we can also discover what God has purposed us to do and become when we read the Word. Respondent H resounded with similar sentiments of many participants with the statement:

I believe He calls them by His Word—according to His Word—for the Bible says in the last days, He's going to pour out His Spirit upon all flesh, and His sons and His daughters shall prophesy, and, of course, 'prophesy' means to preach and proclaim the Word of God, and I believe He calls them by His Word.

Respondent U agreed. This respondent stated, "He says, "Come as you are," so He calls us to ministry, especially according to the Great Commission, "Go ye therefore, and teach all nations..." There was no gender tied to that, so to me, that was generally speaking, to all people."

Respondent D shared, "He calls us through His Word, and we are to be examples when We go out in ministry, sharing what we know about Him in order to draw others to Him. We use His Word and He leads us to Him by His example as well."

Similarly, respondent N stated, "I believe that Jesus calls people into ministry—first of all, their availability but second of all, because of their acceptance of His commission—that we all become ministers through his eyesight..." while respondent I simply stated, "Jesus calls people into ministry through His Word."

Although almost all of the respondents who shared that Jesus calls us to ministry through the Word of God shared their thoughts with high confidence, Respondent P answered, "I guess by studying the Word of God." This respondent expressed less faith in how Jesus calls one into ministry.

Ten of the twenty-two participants discussed the role of the Holy Spirit when being called into the ministry. From this conversation grew several three distinctive themes which included: hearing God's voice, having a passion/gift or purpose, and being led or guided by the Holy Spirit. Although each is a component of being called by the Holy Spirit, each had a unique angle.

Those who discussed hearing the voice of God alluded to the Holy Spirit as being the one who did the calling or speaking. For example, Respondent E concluded, "I believe Jesus calls people into ministry in various ways. Sometimes it can be a burning desire, or it can just be intercommunication—His Spirit into our Spirit so you know it is Him giving you that desire." This respondent described both a voice and a desire or passion. Respondent R simply remarked, "He speaks to them." Respondent K reflected and announced, "I can only speak for how he called me. It was initially hearing the voice of God and having the unction to preach the gospel."

Another function that the participants described was that of one's passion, desire, or abilities as to how the Holy Spirit calls people into ministry.

Respondent C said,

"I believe Jesus calls people into ministry based on what their passion is. I don't believe in just—as far as "pulpit ministry," I believe in the five-fold ministry to include evangelism, teaching, etc. I believe it's developed, actually, in you as a passion. It starts as a passion in you, and I believe that He speaks and once that starts developing—He's developing that passion—that turns into ministry that God has called you to."

Respondent A agreed, "I think it has to be something you're passionate about doing."

Respondent V explained:

"If a person's family is known for music, then a person may feel they're drawn to the music ministry. If you're a family of serving

116

people, servitude may be your ministry. But, sometimes, I feel that we get called not according to what comfortable is, but more so what we'd be uncomfortable with, but God still gives us a heart and mindset and talent to actually excel in what ministry even when we don't think we would be able to, so sometimes it's a matter of what you're comfortable with and then sometimes it'll be what you're uncomfortable with, but God gives you the strength and the knowledge to still execute it."

Respondent B explained,

"He gives a person a gift, and when that person recognizes that gift, that's what He's called them to ... He provides them with everything they need to follow their prospective ministries, and that's how I think it's done. "

Respondent J concluded:

"We have to understand where we fit in the whole scheme of things, and I think He places in each of us a purpose and it's up to us to try to define that purpose with the help of the Holy Spirit. And so, wherever your purpose is, I think that's your ministry."

Three of the participants who expressed the belief that the Holy Spirit calls one into ministry discussed frankly that the Holy Spirit does the calling. Respondents L and G recounted, "Through the Holy Spirit…we are called to ministry." Respondent T recalled,

"Me personally, it [ministry calling] came to me through the Holy Spirit, really. I really didn't have any intention of becoming a minister, but I started going to school, and I thought I'd just be a lecturer. But then God put it upon my mind that this is what He wanted me to do. He just opened a way; he just opened that door. But I was thinking of that. I thought I would just be a teacher at a college or something. So that's why I studied and went back to school. I did this doctorate and that one and a third one."

Sub question 3: How significant is self-help in eradicating gender bias?

Participants in this study interpreted this question differently. Many of whom responded that self-help is very important with little to no explanation; however, of the twenty-two respondents, the two dominant themes emerged: confidence in oneself and obtaining education or knowledge about one's calling. Four respondents discussed needing confidence when considering self-help to eradicate gender bias.

Respondent E explained,

"A lot of women, because of tradition, doubt themselves because of what they have been taught through the years. I think the fact that you're trained and capable of carrying out the ministry that God gives you to do will give you more confidence to go forth."

Respondent C expressed similar sentiments by saying, "Self-help is very significant. I believe you have to be confident in who you are... I think we have to pray and ask God for confidence and to give us the strength to do those things we cannot do. "

Another element of self-help was defined as knowledge and preparedness. Respondents discussed that one should be trained or come to understand the Truth to eradicate gender bias. Another way participants described the element of education is by discussing being prepared and able to push through or pressing forward with what you do know.   Respondent E contended:

"I certainly believe that education is a great tool, so when we go to school and wanted to learn more about God and the doctrines, we were ministering to people to give them Truth, and that is the true Word of God. And so, therefore, we need to stay abreast of current events. A lot of times we say people are not godly, so when we got to school, we are taught what to say and what not to say and how to handle situations."

Respondent J also referred to education being a way to eradicate gender bias in ministry. Respondent J confirmed:

"I think it's very important because if we can't help ourselves to elevate beyond any kind of biases, then we're going to be stuck. And so, it is so important to know who you are and who you belong to, and in knowing that it helps you to understand that you are equal to whatever kind of part in any given situation that God has called you to. "

Respondent P responded, "It's very significant because you want to learn all you can, so in order to learn all you can and do all your research, that's how you find out what is what." Respondent D

119

continued to echo the considerations of others, "It's very important because we can't teach what we don't know." In addition, Respondent B acknowledged the need to eradicate gender bias in ministry through being knowledgeable and prepared.

Respondent B's opinion was:

"In eradicating gender bias, we have to be prepared to what it is that men do, and we have to do it equally as well. The key is knowledge and then pushing through the barriers they exist because of others belief about what you can or cannot do based solely on your gender. In areas that are traditionally male-dominated, women are now pushing through and serving well. But one must have the skills, knowledge and the ability to press through. By so doing, we eradicate gender bias in various arenas of life, including ministry."

Sub-question four: How do gifts of the Holy Spirit make us one?

The dominant theme that emerged from this conversation was the idea that every believer having the Holy Spirit and gifts of the Holy Spirit being on 'one accord.' Although the term inclusion was not explicitly stated, it was inferred throughout the conversations. Twenty-one of the twenty-two participants discussed being unified or one in God because of the Holy Spirit's gifts. Respondent H contended:

"I believe they make us one because even though the gifts are distributed by the Spirit, we are all united into one body by one Lord, one faith, one baptism, one God, the Father, one who's three persons, and the Spirit of God unites us into the Body of Christ. …God is the giver and the Holy Ghost distributes as He sees fit, because that is what the Bible says: He gives gifts according to His heart. It makes us all one, in that if I am called to preach and you're called to teach, that's the Spirit. And, it not only makes us one; it alleviates some of the gender biases because I didn't call myself the preacher. The Holy Ghost did. Just like He called men and he called women to do the same thing. It's His call."

Respondent N commented, "That's what the Lord said—we are one. We are made male and female and He created us as one. The gifts help us to become one so we can become equal."

Respondent N continue to argue that,

"When we are all working towards the same goal, and we're unified by the Holy Spirit, then we will have the same goals and we will not be standing in judgment of anybody else and their belief, but when we're all on the same page and striving to please God, it will come together; it will unify us as one body."

Respondent K reiterated the idea of being one body and everyone operating with gifts of the Spirit, equally. Respondent K shared:

"Again, because there's neither male nor female, Jesus gives those gifts out deliberately to all who seek a gift. And, also, I think it was in the book of Acts that in the last days, He'll pour out His Spirit upon all flesh, and sons and daughters shall prophesy, which means that we will operate under the gifts—young people will have dreams, old will have visions, but we'll operate under the gifts because of the Holy Spirit. He gives to us equally."

Respondent V used a metaphor when addressing this question:

"Gifts are kind of like the gears of the clock. They interconnect in so many different ways and where something may not seem like it will fit in one place, it may fit another place and that fits elsewhere. So are our individual gifts—the goals for our individual gifts and the end-goal of our gifts and different ministries is to help people, to serve people, please God, to further the ministry, then our gifts are always going to be successful, and they're always going to be the right thing. Their end goal, their goal is all on one accord."

Respondents L and T concurred that the gifts make us one and the same because they put us on one accord with God. Respondent T continued, "Nobody's better than anybody else. Nobody's work is more important than anybody else's. We are one."

Respondents O, R, and E agreed. They each discussed how the gifts of the Holy Spirit make us one by bringing everyone into one accord. Respondent O declared, "There are different gifts, but it's just one Spirit giving all the gifts, so it makes us one."

Respondent R stated, "Each person uses his/her gift to work on one accord and that's the thing that pleases the Lord." Respondent E explained, "The gifts support each other. When we combine all of our gifts and abilities, we become one because He gives every church what they need." Respondents P, U and B all stated that gifts connects us and allows us to be on one accord. Specifically, Respondent U confided, "Because we are all connected. The Bible says that we are all on one accord, okay. The Bible even tells us that the Holy Spirit gives us these gifts deliberately as He see fit...."

Although each participant reflected upon experiences of the gifts of the Holy Spirit differently, each participant recognized that it is through the gifting of the Holy Spirit that gender bias diminishes as part of the functionality in the Kingdom of God as each person shares a deep belief that God desires for all people to be on one accord.

Sub-question five: How are women included in the Great Commission?

Of the twenty-two participants, all but one participant expressed the belief that women are included in the Great Commission. The dominant theme from this part of the interview is male and female inclusion in ministry. Participants made delineations between the all-male group selected as disciples of Jesus and the all-inclusive use of the word "ye" that indicates a general term for you, including any person and not just a specific gender. Many of the comments detailed that there is no specific gender targeted; rather, Jesus was talking to everyone.

Respondent S echoed the answer of many by responding, "It doesn't say male or female; it just says "go." Everybody's included." Respondent Q agreed and commented, "Women are included in that because God doesn't say whether it's man or woman. It says anyone can go, women included." Respondent M recounted, "God has poured out His Spirit on sons and daughters alike, and equipping both genders ...with the Great Commission, we all— male and female— have been commissioned to carry God's Word." Respondent F also agreed and stated, "We are included because He did not say male or female; He said, "go," and that can mean that anybody can go. All he wants you to do is go and spread His Word regardless of your gender." Respondent I also bellowed similar beliefs: "Women as well as men can spread the Word. It's not discriminatory from women to men, so everyone is included. Yes, He meant all of us. Not one gender. Just everybody. Respondent K offered, "There's neither male nor female in Christ, and so I do feel that God has called women as well as men." Respondent D also agreed.

"He didn't specify male; He just said, "Go ye therefore, and teach all nations..." so that included everyone. He didn't specify a gender; He said "go," He was talking to everybody, male or female, both, everybody. It was a commission to us all."

Respondents L, G, and A agreed that God included women in the Great Commission. While participants also agreed, they elaborated more about the inclusiveness of women. Respondent O stated, "...I think that it was God's purpose to be an all-inclusive God, and He is not gender-specific when it comes to ministry." Respondent R not only shared a belief that God included women but that women are indeed "equal to men when it comes to the Bible and preaching and teaching the Holy Word." Respondent E felt when Christ gave the command

124

in Matthew 28, "He told all of His disciples to go and teach and spread the gospel, so women are included. It was not gender-specific to men, but it is for the entire Body of Christ." Respondent C reflected,

"I believe that women are included in that because I believe that during Jesus' earthly ministry, He had women around Him and involved in ministry. Women basically supported Him and His ministry. They were used as witnesses of the things He had done. I believe since women were a part of Jesus' ministry from the beginning, that's how we are a part of the Great Commission even now."

Respondent T exclaimed,

Looking at the Great Commission, it said particularly, He was talking to the 11 disciples who went away to Galilee to the mountain where He had appointed them, so this was after the resurrection. And He said, "All power is given unto Me in heaven and in Earth. Go, ye, therefore and teach all nations, baptizing them in the Father, Son, and Holy Spirit, teaching them to observe all things that I've commanded you." He didn't specify that He was only talking to men. To me, it's general. We are all responsible for taking the Word of God into the world. So, He was talking to 11 men and the women who were also around.

Respondent N revealed, "There should not be any place where we cannot go because of our gender; there should be no place where we cannot carry the gospel." Respondent H concluded that "...the Great Commission is a mandate given to all, including women."

Additionally, Respondent J suggested:

"Any part of the Word of God that speaks to humankind, speaks to male and female, and so, when the Great Commission says go, He is assigning everyone who is called into the Body of Christ to go and minister…I don't see a difference."

Conclusion

The researcher conducted a mixed-methods approach to collect, analyze and report data for the study. The hypothesis for this study was: If female ministers at Greater Calvary Missionary Baptist Church receive training on gender equality in ministry, then their knowledge of gender equality would increase. The guiding question for this research was: To what extent are female ministers perceived as equal to male ministers? Sub-questions include the following: 1. Do you believe that there was gender equality when God created mankind? Please explain. 2. How does Jesus call people to ministry? 3. How significant is self-help in eradicating gender bias? 4. How do gifts of the Holy Spirit make us one? And 5. How are women included in the "Great Commission?"

The quantitative and qualitative data revealed similar results, yielding a null hypothesis. The pre/post tests have revealed no statistically significant change in the participants' perception after lessons were given on gender bias or gender equality in ministry. The qualitative data showed that while many people agree with the ideals of women's equality, there are many barriers to realizing women's equality in the church within this context. The guiding question could have been misleading as the participants unanimously agree that women are equal to men; however, the gaps occur in levels of ministry and the extent to which participants believe gender equality is a problem as it now exists within this context.

CHAPTER VI

REFLECTION, SUMMARY, AND CONCLUSION

Being a female minister within the context of this study and having had several experiences in similar ministry denominations, the researcher acknowledges personal growth as a result of the entire process. While personal experiences loaned themselves as a rite of passage within the ministry context, the researcher needed to audit herself to reduce bias. The hypothesis for the study was if female ministers at Greater Calvary Missionary Baptist Church Birmingham receive training on gender equality in ministry, then their knowledge of gender equality would increase. The researcher's approach to this inquiry was a mixed-methods approach. The researcher expected this hypothesis to reveal statistical significance in female perceptions between pre-test and post-test results; however, the results proved a null hypothesis instead.

The researcher used SPSS to conduct a paired T-test in the quantitative section to explore the pre/post-test data [78]. Also, an ANOVA and an Independent T-test was run to analyze demographic data. These reports and graphs show how and where the participants' perceptions differ in five categories: 1. Sex, 2. Age, 3. Education, 4. Leadership Capacity within the church, and 5. Status of Ministry Recognition (license/ordination status). There were 30 participants in the study. Participants completed a pre-test of six demographic questions and 21 quantitative questions using a

1-5 Likert scale is a rating scale used to measure attitudes or opinions. With this scale, respondents were asked to rate items on a level of agreement [78].

Participants then attended six lessons based on several topics regarding the evidence and benefit of women in ministry. After attending the lessons, participants received a post-test survey which contained the same questions as the pre-test.

For the qualitative analysis of this study, the guiding question for this research was: To what extent are female ministers perceived as equal to male ministers? Sub-questions included the following: 1.

Do you believe that there was gender equality when God created mankind? Please explain. 2. How does Jesus call people to ministry? 3. How significant is self-help in eradicating gender bias? 4. How do gifts of the Holy Spirit make us one? And 5. How are women included in the "Great Commission?"

The quantitative and qualitative data revealed similar results, yielding a null hypothesis. The pre/post tests have revealed no statistically significant change in the participants' perception after lessons were given about gender bias. The qualitative data showed that while many agree with the ideals of women's equality, there are many barriers to realizing women's equality in the church within this context. The guiding question could have been misleading as the participants unanimously agree that women are equal to men; however, the gaps occur in levels of ministry and the extent to which participants believe gender equality is a problem as it now exists within this context.

Reflections

Prior to the study, the researcher believed that knowledge was a light that forbids the lingering of ignorance; however, it stands to reason that customs and culture are the traditions that make the Word of God ineffective. This illuminates the need for the ongoing expounding of truth that would wrestle with mindsets to bring liberty and acceptance to a higher truth.

The first session set the tone and raised the bar for the

subsequent sessions. The presenter was very effective in rallying support and interest from the audience. People were clapping, engaging, and responding, "Teach us." This response confirmed the researcher's belief that this study was of interest to the researcher and the attendees. This speaker made the case that God created males and females as equals in dominating the earth and not dominating the other. He also insisted that the fall of mankind in the Garden of Eden created a centerpiece for many who would argue otherwise; having rightly divided the Word of God, the presenter masterfully laid a foundation for participants to make meaningful connections with the premise of the study.

After this session, the researcher reviewed documentation of attendance and began the tedious task of reviewing the pre-test data and combing through the open-ended interview data. The researcher also thought a lot about the first session. It became clearer that this study would impact the researcher's life, and everyone who participated would be impacted positively. No one wanted the class to end. Everyone applauded the speaker and remarked that his presentation excelled their expectations. This sparked an ongoing conversation about snakeology versus theology, the impact of a slave mentality, and other structures that created mindsets in the Black church.

Subsequent lessons continued the momentum of the first meeting. Participants were committed to the process and expressed interest in future meetings. The researcher understood and decoded the actions of the participants' commitment in two ways: 1. They were committed to helping the researcher, and 2. They were interested in knowing more about women in ministry. Even a few of the deacons were present and engaged in the lessons. Everyone was positively engaged and made meaningful connections between their individual beliefs and the collective narrative about inequities in a general term. It is unclear how this information challenged their existing knowledge or impacted their core beliefs.

As the researcher discussed her observations and data with members of her committee, discussions were raised around the central idea of the study. These conversations helped the researcher understand how to capture the energy from the sessions to continue meaningful conversations. These conversations also led to an intimate interview with the Senior Pastor about his perceptions of inequities between males and females in ministry. This conversation helped sharpen the researcher's view of the impact of leadership over the congregation. It also reminded the researcher of the power of the "buy-in" from leadership and how it transferred to the participants feeling safe about sharing and asking questions of the presenters.

In particular, some of the female ministers asked a presenter for wisdom in facilitating a conversation about being included in various aspects of ministry. Another participant asked how to handle it when your gifts are different and not well received within the context. Female ministers expressed desires to be included in ministry services using their spiritual gifts.   These powerful conversations allowed many to voice their concerns, be heard by their peers, and receive helpful tips.

Although the researcher began the study by giving gifts to the participants, such as a journal and ink pens, the researcher was able to do this only once. Afterward, the researcher had meals catered so that the participants would be able to enjoy fellowship as well as engage in learning. The participants responded well to the meals provided and the efforts of the researcher to respect time limits. While the researcher's passion for the subject would be enough to sustain her interest, she understood not everyone shared the same passion. The researcher desired to extend the meetings to ensure everyone had access to each speaker for a question-and-answer session. Some presenters reserved allotted time for that purpose; however, some participants approached the presenter privately to continue conversations.

An important note is the impact the study has had on the researcher. The researcher anticipated hosting and facilitating discussions that would promote awareness regarding gender equity; however, the researcher experienced far more. The academic and spiritual growth was overwhelming. The feeling of offering support to a vulnerable population within this study proved to be needed and widely accepted. From this experience, it was recognized that there was a need to offer support and provide a safe place for female ministers to have a voice as they navigate their way through ministry outlets. As a result of this study, this need was apparent and has now become a passion in the heart of the researcher. This inspiration has conceived a plan to continue the conversations within the context and beyond. In addition to inspiring a very pointed purpose for the researcher, the experience from the research has created a community of female ministers and laypersons who have extended a quest for additional resources and ongoing

> "If I can help somebody as I travel along ...then my living shall not be in vain."

conversations about gender equity and spiritual gifts. The researcher envisions hosting support sessions organized around providing support and mentorship to female ministers who want to be supported and mentored. While this may not create a platform for female ministers, it would propel the researcher to fulfill the desire of a ministry aspiration which is best expressed through lyrics sang by the late great Mahalia Jackson, "If I can help somebody as I travel along ...then my living shall not be in vain." By providing this assistance, the researcher could begin to bridge the gap and continue the conversation about gender equity in church leadership. This alone makes the journey powerful for the researcher and those within the context of this study.

Many presenters are now resources for the community of female ministers who participated in the study. Each presenter has shared contact information and has expressed a willingness to continue teaching upon request. Each presenter demonstrated expertise in various components of understanding and overcoming gender bias and offered supplemental material as additional resources. With this arsenal of resources, the candidate now has a toolkit to selectively use to build upon the foundation that this study has provided.

Moreover, the candidate looked inwardly, outwardly, and upwardly to find meaning and purpose. Inwardly, she discovered that meta-cognitive development is a process. To unlearn and relearn opposing truths requires time, repetitive, and sometimes violent exchange. Teaching adults requires different skills and strategies than teaching children. While all participants were adults, not every adult represented the same level of cognitive development. Outwardly, the researcher discovered that the social construct in which true learning takes place requires trust and confidence. First, the participant must trust that the teacher is honest and confident that what is said is factual, which often means socially acceptable and applicable or relevant to the listeners' here and now. Finally, the candidate looked upward. Remembering the purpose of this study is not driven by the hope of academic achievement alone but by the idea that what is being investigated is meaningful and purposeful and adds to the body of knowledge about God so that it illuminates the truth.

This has been an incredible journey filled with wondrous learning and a tedious task. This study forced the researcher to identify a true passion, develop a community with the context of the study, build interest in the study and measure the impact of teaching and learning. These research findings added expertise to the researcher as a student and as a professional. The collaboration among committee members, as the study continued, guided this study successfully.

As the candidate reflects on the totality of the experience, one may observe that her passion for using her knowledge and expertise to help others is now an ultimate goal. Those who have championed this study and the researcher have also rekindled a fire that would only be quenched when, and only when, the researcher can no longer carry the torch for others as some have done for her. She knows what it is like to be marginalized in the workplace both as a Black, as a female, and in the church as a minister of the Gospel of Jesus Christ. It is with that reality that she has undertaken this project.

Conclusion

From personal experience as a female minister within this context, the researcher believed it was important to investigate gender bias. The hypothesis for this study was if female ministers at Greater Calvary Missionary Baptist Church Birmingham receive training on gender equality in ministry, then their knowledge of gender equality would increase. The researcher employed mixed methods to investigate the hypothesis via a field study.

Existing literature on gender bias in church leadership was scant and very divisive. Many of the resources propagated specific roles for women that differed from men. Those who did usually described women as the "weaker vessel" and men as the head of the house or as a spiritual covering. Others, who disagreed, referred to the Genesis doctrine that describes males and females as having equal authority and domination on the earth. These groups usually added that God has poured his Spirit upon all flesh—including women equal to men—and this outpour of the Holy Spirit is the equalizer. Dr. Ella Mitchell contends that God caused cultural bias breakthroughs where he demonstrated the inclusion of women as equal to that of men in ministry through the works of Jesus Christ [60].

This mixed-methods approach resulted in a null hypothesis. The researcher concluded that while the hypothesis was neither proven nor disproven, completing the study has positively impacted those who participated, including the researcher. The study was both academic and spiritual. The greatest challenge seemed to have been ending the sessions on time. Other barriers were those of long-held teachings about gender that had somehow been pinned in most participants' minds. While the participants verbally communicated the need for gender equity in a whole group setting, when interviewed independently and with others completing individual questionnaires, their responses seemed to contradict what they had communicated during the study. The candidate understands that the cycle of learning requires repetition and the possible group dynamic effects.

Further, she must also consider the emotional and spiritual energy that connects people to a central point during the process, but this energy may not be enough to bring about a lasting change. Unbeknownst to many, this is a common phenomenon in church environments. As a result, the study has concluded the inspiration and aspirations to continue the work of the study have not yielded desired results. The researcher hopes that progress will be realized over time and by faith, if not in this generation, then the next.

Although this study resulted in a null hypothesis, the researcher recommends anyone wishing to complete a similar study considers extending the training sessions. Including the Senior Pastor and church officials in the study creates buy-in and reduces the possibility of creating rifts that such a sensitive subject could create. The researcher also suggests that participants in future studies may require supplemental material that they could continue studying in between sessions that would require them to read and research to enhance conversations and increase relevance.

Finally, this study required much thoughtfulness and consideration from each participant. Having the responsibility to lead in a Christian setting, the researcher acknowledged that the greatest gain was to further promote the gospel of Jesus according to the Scriptures.

APPENDIX A

CONSENT FORM

VIRGINIA UNIVERSITY OF LYNCHBURG

School of Religion

2058 Garfield Avenue

Lynchburg, VA 24501

Doctor of Ministry Research Consent Form

Topic: Gender Equality in Church Ministry

Participants are asked to read this document and ask any question he/she may have before agreeing to be in this study.

Beverly Barnes-McDonald is a degree candidate for the Doctor of Ministry at Virginia University of Lynchburg.

Background Information:

The guiding question for the research is: To what extent is gender bias accepted in church ministry? The problem is that traditionally, clergy females have not experienced equal opportunities as male clergy. The hypothesis is: If female ministers at Greater Calvary Missionary Baptist Church would receive training on gender equality in ministry, then their knowledge in gender equality would increase.

Procedures:

Individual interview sessions will be videotaped using pre-script questions; a follow-up interview will be conducted via phone, face to face and/or using technology such as Skype. All interviews will be recorded and offered to participants for member checking. Data will then be stripped of all identifying information and analyzed for findings.

Risks and Benefits:

The study has no physical component and minimal risk of physical injury. Your participation in this study will be constituted as a contribution to educational research on the perception of gender equality in ministry.

Confidentiality:

The information of this study will be kept private. The researcher will remove all identifying information for publication. Audio and video taped sessions which are used for educational purposes will be used to generate manuscripts and erased at the completion of this study. Your information for the study, however, may be reviewed by the representatives of Virginia University of Lynchburg.

Voluntary Nature of the Study:

Your decision to participate will not affect your current or future relations with the institution of Virginia University of Lynchburg.

Contacts and Questions:

If you should have any questions about your participation in this study or this institution and its connection to this project, please contact the researcher. If you have questions later, you may also contact the researcher at (757) 630-0256. If you want to talk to someone other than the researcher, you may contact a faculty member at Virginia University of Lynchburg, School of Religion. If you decided to participate, know that you are free to withdraw at any time without affecting relationships.

Statement of Consent

(You will be given a copy of this form to keep for your records).

I, _____, have read the above information. I have asked questions and have received answers. I consent to participate in this study.

Signature_____

Date_____

APPENDIX B

LESSON PLANS

Lesson 1: "The Biblical Perspective of Gender Difference: Was there Gender Equality

when God Created Mankind?"

Key scripture: Genesis 1:26-27

Then God said, "Let us make mankind in our image, in our likeness, so that they may rule over the fish in the sea and the birds in the sky, over the livestock and all the wild animals, and over all the creatures that move along the ground." 27So God created mankind in his own image, in the image of God he created them; male and female he created them.

What is gender equality?

Gender equality—A set of actions, attitudes, and assumptions that provide opportunities and create expectations about individuals; the process of allocating resources, programs, and decision-making fairly to both males and females without any discrimination on the basis of sex...and addressing any imbalances in benefits available to males and females [66].

This explains that they were made in the image of God. Subtext: Genesis 5:2, Male and female created He them. And on the day, they were created, He called them "man" Genesis 5:2 and supporting text: Galatians 3:28. As an introduction to the idea of spiritual equality, these foundational scriptures will shape the understanding of the term "man." Participants will be asked to understand that the term man is not to describe domestic roles, rather to address the nature of creation that separates humanity from other creation. This distinction implies that while the male was created first, and the woman taken from a male's rib, God did not create an inferior or superior creation by design. Rather, God created the two to complement for purpose. Phyllis Trible [83] writes:

> From the beginning the word mankind or humankind is synonymous with the phrase "male and female." The parallelism between and male and female shows further that sexual differentiation does not mean hierarchy but rather equality. Created simultaneously male and female are not superior and subordinate. Neither has power over the other, in fact, both are given equal power. Male and female were made in the image of God.

> Male and female are treated equally, neither given dominion over the other. God does not identify himself with sexuality. Sexual differentiation of humankind is not a description of God. It depicts male and female in freedom and uniqueness and upholds the transcendence of the deity of God [83].

However, the Bible does highlight female and male imagery for God.

Lesson points:

1. God created mankind equally.

2. The term mankind includes both male and female.

3. The fall of mankind in the Hebrew culture became a catalyst for male dominance.

Lesson 2: "The Struggles of Women: Setting the Captives Free."

Key scripture: Luke 4:18.

"The Spirit of the Lord is on me because He has anointed me to preach..."

Subtext: John 10:10, Numbers 27. This exploration of scripture questions the cultural bondages of mankind and dares to challenge one to explore the question of spiritual inequality between genders as a form of bondage. The daughters of Zelophehad and their request to Moses that they be given their father's inheritance in Numbers 27 will be explored. This lesson will also dive deeply into the text, Righteous Discontent by Evelyn Higginbotham to examine the barriers women have had to face in different facets of leadership, particularly in the church. Keeping in mind that gender equality is:

Gender equality—A set of actions, attitudes, and assumptions that provide opportunities and create expectations about individuals; the process of allocating resources, programs, and decision-making fairly to both males and females without any discrimination on the basis of sex…and addressing any imbalances in benefits available to males and females [66].

Lesson Points:

1. The role of Black females in the collective ethos of racial self-help is significant to enact change in the lives of Black people.

2. Eradicating gender bias in church frees women to minister.

3. The Spirit of the Lord empowers women to preach.

Lesson 3: The Ministry Calling of Jesus: "Understanding How Jesus Calls People to Ministry."

Key scripture: Mark 16:9. Mary Magdalene was the one to first witness Jesus' resurrection and was given the charge to go and tell others.

Subtext: Luke 8:2. Mary Magdalene was one of the ones who accompanied Jesus, and some have referred to her as equal to the apostles. She was also one of many women who ministered to and with Jesus as well as to have directly benefited from the ministry of Jesus. Paul urges others to care for the females who "co-labored" in the gospel with him Philippians 4:3. God calls to Deborah in Old Testament, Book of Judges. Women were among the seventy-two sent out, Luke 10:1-11.

Lesson Points:

1. Women were included in the sharing of the gospel.

2. The call to ministry is unique to the will and purposes of God, not man.

3. The call of ministry is heard through various circumstances and situations.

Lesson 4: "Vessels and Gifts of the Holy Spirit, Pt.1".

Key scripture: 1 Corinthians 12:4-11.

Subtext: Ephesians 4:11-16. This text will be used to help participants reframe ideas of how the Holy Spirit ministers and through whom the Holy Spirit may minister. This lends itself to understanding that it is indeed the Holy Spirit who ministers through humanity and not vice versa which expands the ministry of the Holy Spirit to whosoever is yielded and obedient.

Lesson Points:

1. There are a variety of spiritual gifts which are given by God's Holy Spirit.

2. The gifts of the Holy Spirit are not bound by gender.

3. The gifts of the Holy Spirit make us one.

Lesson 5: "Vessels and Gifts of the Holy Spirit, Pt .2."

148

Key scripture: 2 Timothy 2:21.

Subtext: Galatians 3:28. This text will be used to help participants reframe ideas of how the Holy Spirit ministers and through whom the Holy Spirit may minister. This lends itself to understanding that it is indeed the Holy Spirit who ministers through humanity and not vice versa which expands the ministry of the Holy Spirit to whosoever is yielded and obedient.

Lesson Points:

1. Gifts of the Spirit are given to men and women, equally.

2. God used women in leadership.

3. Women of the early church operate in spiritual gifts as they do today.

Lesson 6: "The Great Commission."

Key scripture: Matthew 28:19-20. The commission given from Jesus to Believers is to expand the Kingdom of God through teaching, discipleship and baptism. This commission is not aimed at a particular gender, but it is inclusive of people. This lesson will compel listeners to consider how the customs of the Old Testament shape our beliefs in women's roles and responsibilities in the Kingdom of God compared to New Testament practices.

Lesson Points:

1. Women were included in the "Great Commission."

2. Women were empowered by the Spirit of God.

3. Women had a significant role in the growth of the church.

APPENDIX C

GRAPHS DISPLAYING

QUANTITATIVE DATA

Sex Demographics (n=30)

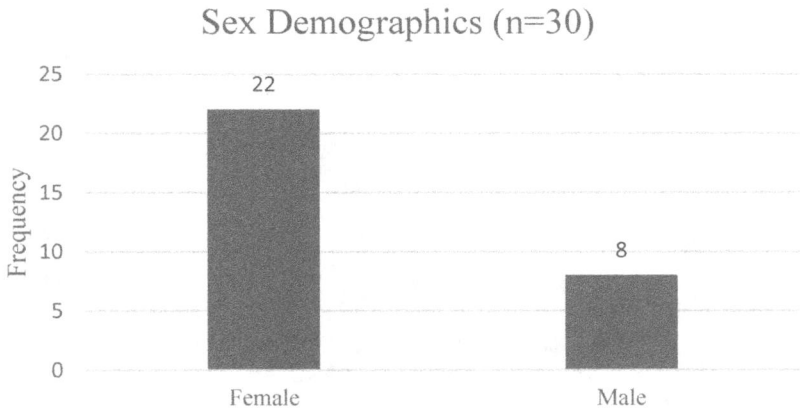

Graph One - Demographics of participants based on sex.

Education Demographics (n=30)

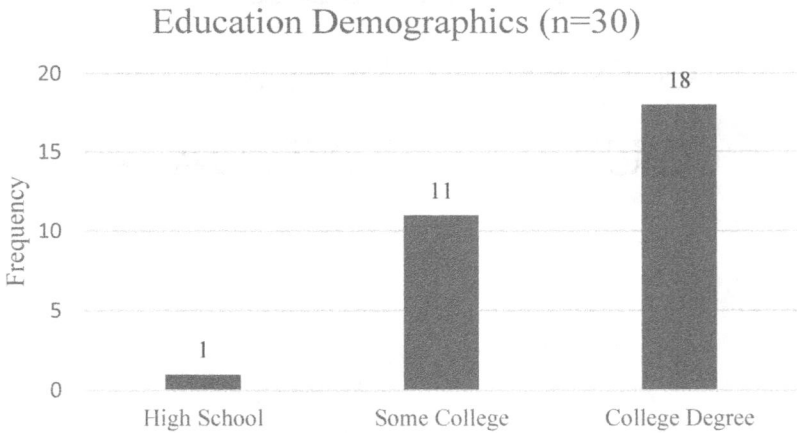

Graph Two - Demographics of participants based on education level.

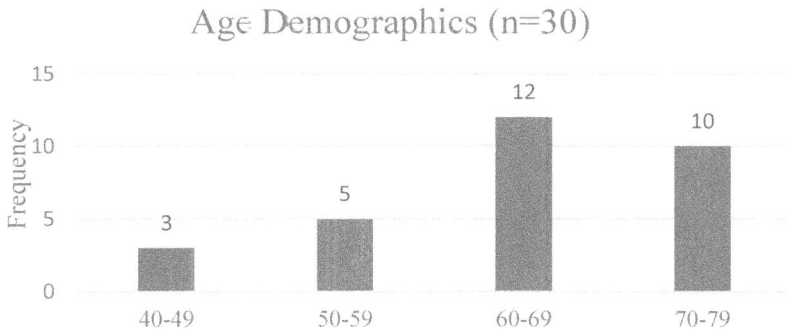

Graph Three Demographics of participants based on age range.

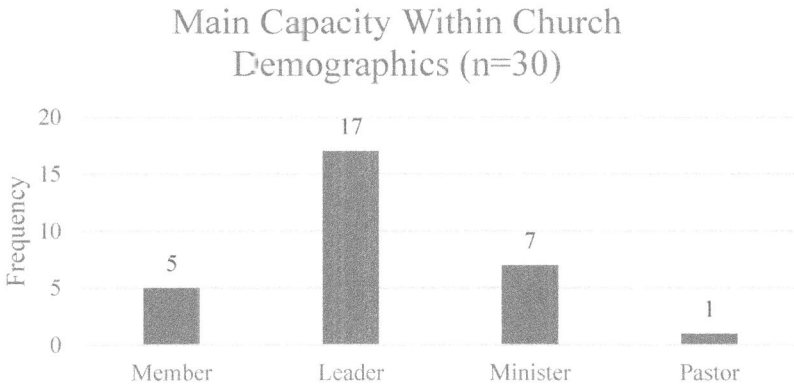

Graph Four - Demographics based on the participants position and capacity they serve within the church.

153

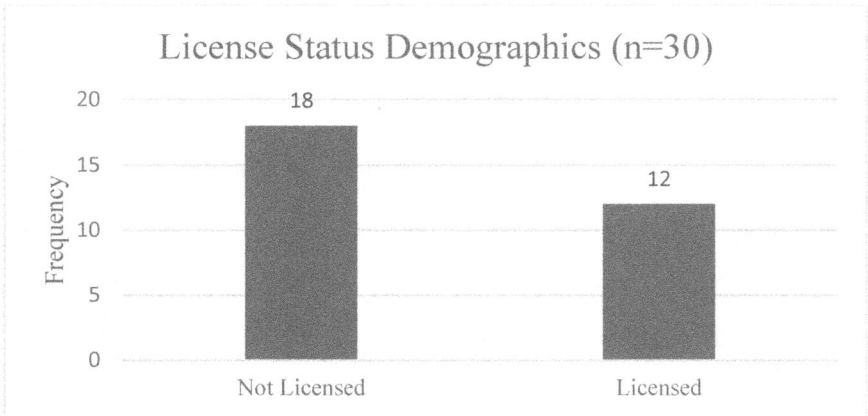

License Status Demographics (n=30)

Graph Five - Demographics based on licensed church leader status of participants.

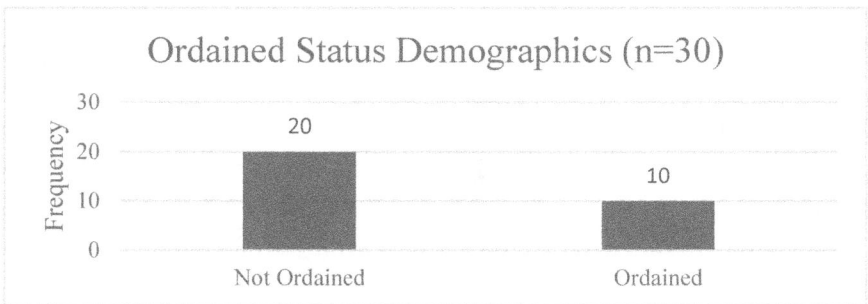

Ordained Status Demographics (n=30)

Graph Six - Demographics based on ordained church leader status of participant.

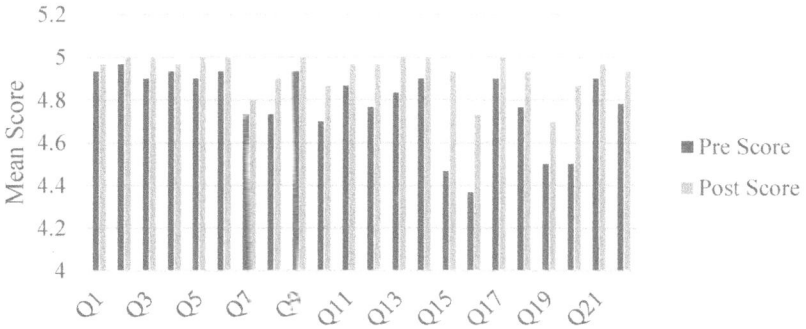

Comparisons of Pre-Test and Post-Test
Scores for Questions 1-21 and Overall

Graph Seven - Double bar graph comparing pre-test and post-test
means for each question and the cumulative mean for all questions.

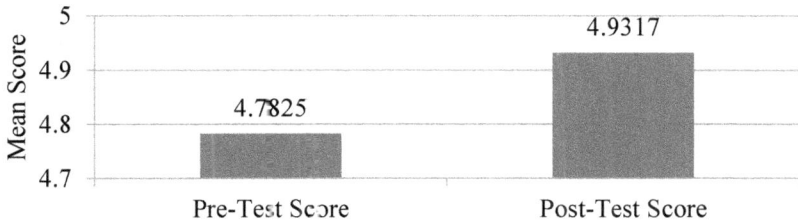

Comparison of Cumulative Pre-Test and
Post-Test Means

Graph Eight - Comparison of the cumulative means of all pre-test
and post-test questions.

155

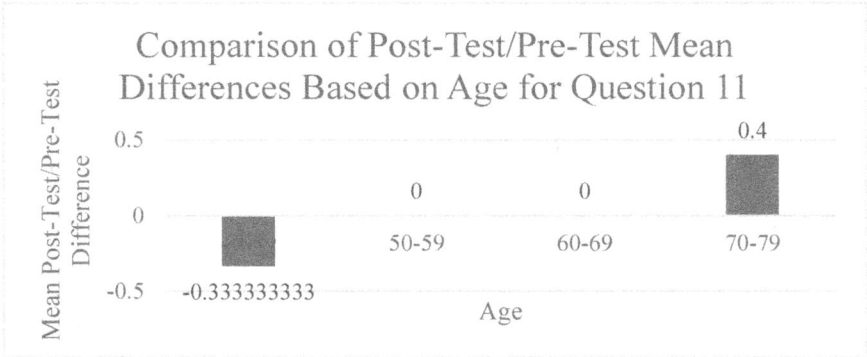

Graph Nine - Mean of each age group's pre-test/post-test difference for Question 11.

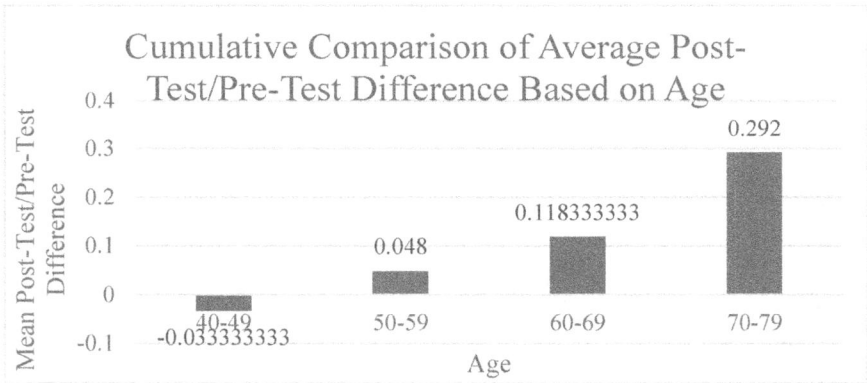

Graph Ten - Cumulative mean of each age group's Pre-Test/Post-Test difference.

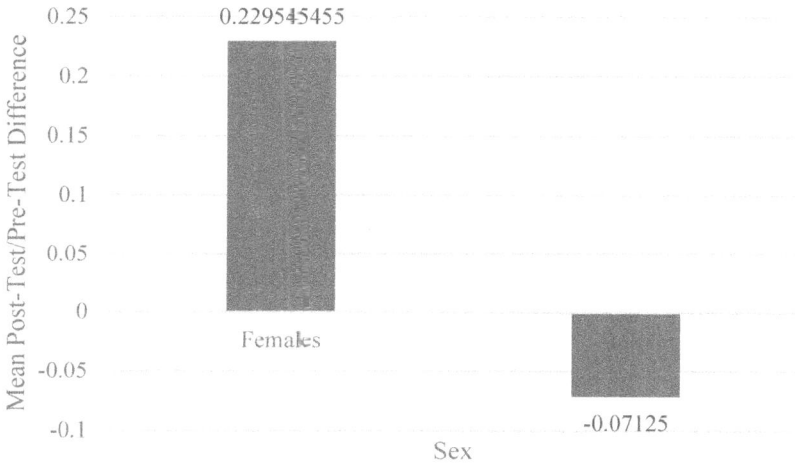

Cumulative Comparison of Average Post-Test/Pre-Test Difference Based on Sex

Graph 11 Mean Differences by Sex.

APPENDIX D
INTERVIEW INSTRUMENTS

Below are the questions guiding the research and the sub-questions each participant will be asked using a semi-structured format.

There is one central question that guides this research: To what extent is gender bias accepted in church ministry? Sub-questions include the following:

1. Was there gender-equality when God created mankind?

2. How does Jesus call people to ministry?

3. How significant is self-help in eradicating gender bias?

4. How do gifts of the Holy Spirit make us one?

5. How are women included in the "Great Commission?"

Quantitative Instrument

Pre/post test

Section I. Demographics.

1. Please indicate your age range.

○ 20-39   ○40-49   ○50-59   ○60-69   ○70-79

2. Identify your gender

○Male ○Female

3. Please indicate the capacity you serve in church. Select all that applies.

○Member ○Leader ○Minister ○Pastor

4. Are you licensed as a church leader in any capacity?

○ Yes   ○No

5. Are you ordained as a church leader in any capacity?

○ Yes   ○No

6. Please select the highest level of school completed.

○Some High School ○High School ○Some College○ College Degree

Please continue to the next section.

Section II.

Please select your best choice in response to each statement.

Strongly agree=5, agree=4, neither agree nor disagree=3, disagree=2, or strongly disagree=1.

1. Gifts of the Holy Spirit are available to males and females, equally.

○5 ○4 ○3 ○2 ○1

2. The Holy Spirit uses men and women to preach.

○5 ○4 ○3 ○2 ○1

3. God calls women to ministry.

o5 o4 o3 o2 o1

4. The Great Commission is given to men and women.

o5 o4 o3 o2 o1

5. The Holy Spirit empowers women to minister to all people.

o5 o4 o3 o2 o1

6. Women can teach to males and females.

o5 o4 o3 o2 o1

7. Men and women are equal in ministry.

o5 o4 o3 o2 o1

8. Women face more challenges in ministry than men.

o5 o4 o3 o2 o1

9. Women can be spiritual leaders in church.

o5 o4 o3 o2 o1

10. The Bible supports women as leaders in the church.

o5 o4 o3 o2 o1

11. There are examples of women leadership in the Bible.

o5 o4 o3 o2 o1

12. God calls females to ministry, not just males.

o5 o4 o3 o2 o1

13. God uses various situations/circumstances to call people into ministry.

o5 o4 o3 o2 o1

14. Mankind is a biblical term which includes male and female.

o5 o4 o3 o2 o1

15. God created male and female equally.

o5 o4 o3 o2 o1

16. Male dominance in the Bible is a result of the fall of mankind and Hebrew culture.

o5 o4 o3 o2 o1

17. The Spirit of the Lord empowers women to preach.

o5 o4 o3 o2 o1

18. Gender bias must be eradicated so women can freely minister.

o5 o4 o3 o2 o1

19. Women of the early church operated in spiritual gifts as women do today.

o5 o4 o3 o2 o1

20. Women played a significant role in the growth of the early church.

○5 ○4 ○3 ○2 ○1

21. Women are included in the "Great Commission."

○5 ○4 ○3 ○2 ○1

BIBLIOGRAPHY

1) Adler, Emily Stier, and Roger Clark. An Invitation to Social Research: How it's Done. Belmont: Wadsworth Publishing, 2003.

2) Akbar, Na'im. Breaking the Chains of Psychological Slavery. Tallahassee: Mind Productions & Associates, 1996.

3) Ammerman, Nancy T., Jackson W. Carroll, Carl S. Dudley, and William McKinney. Studying Congregations. Nashville: Abingdon Press, 1998.

4) Anders, Max E. and Judith A. Lunsford. 30 Days to Understand Church History. Brentwood: Wolgemuth & Hyatt Publishers, 1991.

5) Anderson, Tyree. "The Ministry Calling of Jesus: Understanding How Jesus Calls People to Ministry." 2019.

6) The Austin Stone Community Church. What is the Role of Women in the Church?, https:// www.church clarity.org/church/Austin-Stone community Church-374.

7) Baldwin, Lewis V. There Is a Balm in Gilead: The Cultural Roots of Martin Luther King, Jr. Minneapolis: Fortress Press, 1991.

8) Barna, George. The Power of Team Leadership: Achieving Success through Shared Responsibility. Colorado Springs: WaterBrook, 2001.

9) Bates, Gerri. Alice Walker: A Critical Companion. Greenwood Press. https://www.worldcat.org/oclc/62321382. (accessed May 10, 2018).

10) Bethel Missionary Baptist Church, Pratt City archives. (Accessed February 17, 2016).

11) Billingsley, Andrew. Mighty Like a River: The Black Church and Social Reform. Oxford: Oxford University Press, 1999.

12) Briggs, J.R., and Eugene H. Peterson. Fail: Finding Hope and Grace in the Midst of Ministry Failure. Downers Grove: InterVarsity Press, 2014.

13) Brown, Brene'. Rising Strong: How The Ability To Reset Transforms The Way We Live, Love, Parent, and Lead. New York City: House Trade, 2017.

14) Bryant, Charles V. Rediscovering Our Spiritual Gifts: Building Up the Body of Christ Through the Gifts of the Spirit. Nashville: Upper Room, 1991.

15) Burroughs, Ernest. Dissertation Paper: Eradicating Gender Bias in Church Leadership, Darlington, SC, 2005.

16) Burroughs, Nannie Helen. Journal of the National Baptist Convention, 1900. M286.N21.

17) Calagna, Steve. Women in Ministry. A Theological Position Paper. King's Seminary, 2003.

18) Cannon, Katie G. Womanism and the Soul of the Black Community. New York: Continuum Press, 1996. Coleman, James E., Jr. "The Gender Difference: Was There Gender Equality When God Created Mankind?" 2019.

19) Coleman, James. The Biblical Perspective of Gender Difference: Was There Gender Equality When God Created Mankind? 2019.

20) Cone, James. Liberation, A Black Theology of Liberation. Philadelphia: J.B. Lippincott Company, 1970.

21) Creswell, John W. Research Design Qualitative & Quantitative Approaches. London: Sage Publications, 1994.

22) Davidson, Richard M., Women in Ministry: Headship, Submission, and Equality in Scripture. SDA Theological Seminary, 2016. https://www.sdanet.org/atissuebooks/wim/wim13dav.htm. (accessed December 5, 2017).

23) Derensborurg, Edwin. The Liberated Mind: Throwing off the Bonds of the Past and Finding Freedom in Christ. Rockville: Pneuma Life Publishing, 1997.

24) Easton, MG. Illustrated Bible Dictionary, 3rd Edition, Thomas-Nelson, 1897.

25) Evans, James. We Have Been Believers. Minneapolis: Fortress Press, 1992.

26) Study Bible: English Standard Version (ESV). Wheaton, Ill: Crossway Bibles, 2007.

27) Fortune, Marie M, and James N. Poling. Sexual Abuse by Clergy: A Crisis for the Church. Eugene: Wipf & Stock, 2004.

28) Freeman, Lindsay Harbin. Bible Women: All Their Words and Why They Matter. Philadelphia: NavPress Publishing Group, 2014.

29) Fullan, Michael. The Six Secrets of Change. San Francisco: Jossey-Bass, 2008.

30) Garrison, Greg. "'We Had to Take Care of the People': Pratt City Church Rebuilt Three Years After 2011 Tornado." Alabama Media Group, 2014.

31) Gilkes, Cheryl. If it Wasn't for the Women: Black Women's Experience and Womanist Culture in Church and Community. Maryknoll, Orbis Book, 2002.

32) Greenwood, Davydd J., and Morten Levin. Introduction to Action Research: Social Research for Social Change. London Oaks: Sage Publications, 1998.

33) Griggs, Donald L. Teaching Teachers to Teach: A Basic Manual for Church Teachers. Nashville: Abingdon Press, 1980.

34) Hagin, Kenneth E. The Woman Question. Tulsa: RHEMA Bible Church, 1983.

35) Hamon, Jane. The Deborah Company. Santa Beach: Christian International Family Church, 1999.

36) Harris, James H. Pastoral Theology: A Black Church Perspective. Minneapolis: Fortress Press, 1991.

37) Heald, Cynthia. Becoming a Woman of Purpose. Carol Stream: Tyndale House Publishers, 2014.

38) Higginbotham, Evelyn Brooks. Righteous Discontent: The Women's Movement in the Black Baptist Church 1880-1920. Cambridge: Harvard University Press, 1994.

39) Historical Society Archives. Two Industrial Towns: Pratt City and Thomas, https://www.bhistorical.org/pdf/Pratt%20City_Thomas.pdf. (Accessed August 9, 2016).

40) Houghtby-Haddon, Natalie K. Changed Imagination, Changed Obedience: Social Imagination and the Bent-Over Woman in the Gospel of Luke. New York: Pickwick Publication, 2011.

41) Hollies, Linda H. Inner Healing for Broken Vessels. Nashville: Upper Room Books, 1992.

42) Holy Bible. The King James (KJ) Study Bible. Thomas Nelson Publishers Inc., 1988.

43) Holy Bible. The New Scofield Study Bible. New York, Oxford University Press.

44) Hopkins, Dwight N. Down, Up, and Over: Slave Religion and Black Theology. Minneapolis: Fortress Press, 2000.

45) Hopkins, Dwight, Introducing Black Theology of Liberation. Mary Knoll: Orbis Book, 1999.

46) Jarrett, Pam. Now is the Time. Bloomington: AuthorHouse Publishing, 2013.

47) Jones, Kirk Byron. Rest in the Storm: Self-Care Strategies for Clergy and Other Caregivers. Valley Forge: Judson Press, 2001.

48) Kapolyo, Joe M. The Human Condition: Christian Perspective through African Eyes. Downers Grove: InterVarsity Press, 2005.

49) King, Jeanne Porter. "How to Deal with Sexism in Your Church, "CBE International, https://www.cbeinternational.org/blogs/how-deal-sexism-your-church (accessed February 2, 2020).

50) Kitt, Zelda. Vessels and the Gifts of the Holy Spirit: Part I and II, 2019.

51) Kumar, Ranjit. Research Methodology: A Step-by-Step Guide for Beginners, 3rd Edition. Thousand Oaks: Sage Publication, 2005.

52) Leggett, Glenn C., David Mead, and William Charvat. Prentice-Hall Handbook for Writers 7th edition. New Jersey: Prentices Hall, 1978.

53) Lewis, Jone Johnson. "Biography of Maria W. Stewart, Activist and Abolitionist, ThoughtCo.", https://www.thoughtco.com/maria-stewart-biography-3530406 (accessed February 5, 2020).

54) Liardon, Robert. God's Generals. Why They Succeeded and Why Some Fail. Tulsa: Albury Publishing, 1996.

55) Life Application Bible. New International Version. Wheaton & Grand Rapids: Tyndall House Publishers, Inc. & Zondervan Publishing House, 1995.

56) Lincoln, C. Eric, and Lawrence H. Mamiya. The Black Church in the African American Experience. Durham: Duke University Press, 1991.

57) Marciniak, Barbara. Bringers of the Dawn. Edited by Tera Thomas. Rochester: Bear & Company Publishing, 1992.

58) Mays, Marshall D. SERVING TOGETHER: The Pastor and deacon in Cooperation, Not Conflict. Lynchburg: 2018.

59) McKenzie, Vashti M. Not Without a Struggle: Leadership Development for African American Women in Ministry. Cleveland: United Church Press, 1996.

60) Mitchell, Ella Pearson. Those Preaching' Women, Sermons by Black Women Preachers. Vol 1. Valley Forge: Judson Press, 1991.

61) Mitchell, Ella Pearson. Women: To Preach or Not To Preach, 21 Outstanding Black Preacher Say Yes! Valley Forge: Judson Press, 1991.

62) Mitchem, Stephanie Y. Introducing Womanist Theology. Maryknoll: Orbis Books, 2002.

63) Moore, Geraldine. "The Struggles of Women: Setting the Captives Free." 2019.

64) Myers, William. God's Yes it Louder than My No: Rethinking the African Call to Ministry and the Irresistible Urge to Preach: A Collection of African America "Call" to ministry and the "call" Stories. Trenton: Africa World Press, 1994.

65) New Scofield Study Bible (NIV), New York, Oxford University Press.

66) Nzewi, Uchenna Mariestella. "Women participation in Science , Technology, Engineering and Mathematics (STEM) for National Development." Women and Development 9, no. 4 (January 2016): 66-92., https://www.researchgate.net/publication/315378700 (accessed March 11, 2020).

67) Pace, Courtney Freedom Faith: The Womanist Vision of Prathia Hall. Athens: University of Georgia Press, 2019.

68) Pfeiffer, Charles. The Dead Sea Scrolls and the Bible. Grand Rapids: Baker Books, 1969.

69) Reavis, Ralph. Two Paths to Freedom. Richmond: African American Publishers of Virginia, 2000.

70) Ree, Erik. S.H.A.P.E., Finding and Fulfilling Your Unique Purpose for Life. Grand Rapids: Zondervan, 2006.

71) Reid, E.R. The Proverbs 31 Woman: A Study Aid. Shippensburg: Destiny Image Publishers, 1999.

72) Roman, Sanaya. Personal Power through Awareness. Tiburon: H J Kramer, Inc., 1986.

73) Ross, Rosetta. Witnessing and Testifying: Black Women, Religion and Civil Rights. Minneapolis: Fortress Press, 2003.

74) Ryrie, Charles Caldwell. The Role of Women in the Church. Nashville: B&H Publishing, 2011.

75) Sensing, Tim, Qualitative Research: A Multi-Methods Approach to Purpose of Ministry Theses. Eugene: Wipf Stock Publication, 2011.

76) Smiley, Tavis, and Cornel West. The Covenant in Action. 1st ed. Carlsbad: Smiley Books, 2007.

77) Southern Baptist Convention. (2000). from Southern Baptist Convention:, https://www.sbc.net/bfm2000/bfm2000.asp (accessed December 23, 2016).

78) SPSS, https://spss.en.softonic.com. (accessed October 4, 2019).

79) Stevenson Moessner. Through the Eyes of Women: Insights for Pastoral Care. Minneapolis: Fortress Press, 1996.

80) Strong, James. Strong Exhaustive Concordance of the Bible. Abingdon Press.

81) Thayer, Joseph H. Thayer's Greek-English Lexicon of the New Testament. Grand Rapids: Baker, 1970.

82) Tiffany, Frederick C. and Sharon H. Ringe. Biblical Interpretation: A Roadmap. Nashville: Abingdon Press, 1996.

83) Trible, Phyllis. God and the Rhetoric of Sexuality. Philadelphia: Fortress Press: 1978.

84) Turabian, Kate, John Grossman, and Alice Bennett. A Manual for Writers of Term Papers, Theses, and Dissertations, 7th edition. Chicago: University of Chicago Press, 1996.

85) Virginia University of Lynchburg, School of Religion, Doctor of Ministry Manual (2017-2019).

86) Vyhmeister, Nancy Jean and Terry Dawain Robertson. Quality Research Papers for Students of Religion and Theology. Grand Rapid: Zondervan, 2014.

87) Walker, David, and Peter P. Hinks. David Walker's Appeal: To the Coloured Citizens of the World. University Park: Pennsylvania State University Press, 2000.

88) Walker, Wyatt T. Somebody's Calling My Name. Valley Forge: Judson Press, 1979.

89) Wells, Ronald. History and the Christian Historian. Grand Rapids: W.B. Eerdmans Publishing , 1998.

90) Willimon, William H. The Theology and Practice of Ordained Ministry, Revised Edition. Nashville: Abingdon Press, 2010.

91) Wheatley, Phyllis, A Hymn to Humanity. www.poemhunter.com. (accessed February 14, 2020).

92) Wilmore, Gayraud S Black Religion and Black Radicalism: An Interpretation of the Religious History of African Americans. Maryknoll: Orbis Books, 1998.

93) Wilson, Teisha. "Jarena Lee (1783–185?), "Black Past, www.blackpast.org/African-American history/lee-Jarena-1783 (accessed February 1, 2020).

94) Wimberly, Edward P. Relational Refugees Alienation and
Reincorporation in African American Churches and
Communities. Nashville: Abingdon Press, 2000.

95) Women 'Take Care,' Men 'Take Charge' – Stereotyping of
U.S. Business Leaders Exposed,
www.catalyst.org/research/women-take-care-men-take-
charge-stereotyping-of-u-s-business-leaders-exposed
(accessed May 12, 2019).

www.ingramcontent.com/pod-product-compliance
Lightning Source LLC
Chambersburg PA
CBHW072005090426
42740CB00011B/2102